TRAINING
for
NON-TRAINERS
A Do-It-Yourself Guide for Managers

Carolyn Nilson

amacom
AMERICAN MANAGEMENT ASSOCIATION

Library of Congress Cataloging-in-Publication Data

Nilson, Carolyn
     Training for non-trainers : a do-it-yourself guide for managers
Carolyn Nilson.
          p.   cm.
     Includes bibliographical references.
     ISBN 0-8144-5974-9
     ISBN 0-8144-7775-5 (pbk.)
     1. Employees—Training of.   I. Title.
HF5549.5.T7N527   1990   89-81025
658.3'124—dc20   CIP

First AMACOM paperback edition 1991.

Printing number

10   9   8

TRAINING
FOR
NON-TRAINERS

Contents

Preface

If you are a manager or supervisor, you are—or should be—a trainer. Whether you manage one employee or hundreds, you probably understand that training can increase employee productivity and contribute significantly to corporate profitability. But you probably do *not* have a professional training background.

How, then, can you acquire the skills and knowledge you must have to train your people? How do you know when you need outside help and where to find it? How can you determine training costs and benefits?

This book will help you. Written mainly for first- and mid-level managers, it is designed as a practical tool for anyone who needs to train people but does not have the expertise of a professional trainer.

Training for Non-Trainers will show you that training doesn't have to be expensive, and that you can often do it yourself. This book will help you to make the right decisions about the most effective kinds of training for many different situations. It will lead you by examples and common sense through the essentials of training design and delivery.

Training for Non-Trainers will show you how to do one-to-one training, peer training, training for groups of employees, and long-distance training. It will give you some insight into how to work effectively and to your benefit with corporate training departments, outside consultants, and external training service providers. Throughout the book, the proven fundamentals of training are emphasized. Examples of specific work situations show you how to apply training principles. Each chapter contains a checklist to help you remember key issues and processes as you plan and implement your own training.

This book will be useful to managers in companies that are too small to hire training professionals, to managers in major corporations who must still do their own training in many situations, to managers who want to work more effectively with their training departments or with outside consultants, and to managers who aren't quite sure whether they need training in the first place. It will also be useful to human resources professionals who must often assume the role of trainer.

Training for Non-Trainers is a strategic resource that will make the manager's job a little easier by demonstrating how to use the tool of effective training. It is for any manager who believes in the power of human resources.

TRAINING
FOR
NON-TRAINERS

CHAPTER 1

How Training Makes Employees More Productive

Training plays an important part in developing a productive work force and in getting operations finely tuned so they can contribute more directly to profits. This chapter explains the relationships between training and productivity, quality, motivation, and communications. It shows you what to consider when you think your employees need training, and it helps you to design useful and appropriate training methods that don't waste time.

The Importance of Training

Training is one major approach to helping people control or manage change. This happens because training is designed to lead the trainee to master new knowledge, attitudes, and skills. A person leaves training with the confidence that he can cope with change. Training is a way of organizing information and experience so that an employee can behave differently on the job—to his own and the company's benefit. Training can be a manager's most efficient strategic tool for enabling employees to take charge of change.

Who Needs It?

All kinds of working people will at some point or other need training. This is because over time organizations change, techniques, equipment, and knowledge change, and people change. Whether they are executives, managers, supervisors or secretaries, technical specialists, production workers, scientists, artists, doctors, lawyers, instructors, security guards, clerks, salespersons, or custodial workers, all at some time will need to know new information, acquire new skills, and develop new attitudes to successfully master the changes in their work environment.

Managers who are responsible for the effectiveness of the work force must recognize that no one is exempt from the need for training. Good training happens when a specific learning experience is designed for a specific worker or worker group. When you think about delivering training, think first about exactly who it is that will be your student.

Think, as you design your training, that good training is like good marketing: It is an organized, step-by-step, coordinated system whose goal is behavior change. Sales don't just happen, and learning doesn't just happen either.

In marketing, you begin with a basic information need and progress through key steps carefully calculated to result in a customer's buying a product or adopting a process. In training, you also begin with a basic information need and progress through well-designed steps to mastery of the learning that leads to change. Like marketing, training is best approached as a hierarchical collection of ideas and procedures that are specific and focused on the accumulation and assimilation of small behavioral changes that lead to greater changes.

What's Special About Adult Learners?

Adults at work who learn new things learn best by relating what's new to what is already part of their experience. Unlike children, who can be compared to blank pages waiting to be filled or sponges ready to absorb, adults bring to the learning situation a vast storehouse of information, of knowledge gained by trial and error, of patterned responses, of approaches that work for them, and of comfortable learning styles. Adults differ from children in the very important area of experience base—and that's critical to making training "stick."

Training that considers this difference and that focuses on relating what is new to what is most likely in the experience base of the adult learner is training that will be successful. Trainers who take the time to find out exactly what jobs their students have and how their training might be applied are trainers who will be successful.

What to Do First

Your first task as a manager is to precisely define your employees' training needs. For example, two word processing specialists need to learn how to create data bases; one word processing specialist needs to know how to import graphic files into text; five chemical engineers need to learn to apply the new formula to their various operations; twenty software evaluators need to learn interpersonal skills to deal with their designers more effectively; fifty retail clerks newly employed for the holiday season need to know how to fill out time sheets and how to charge personal purchases.

The second task is to figure out the best way to present the training information to each employee so that only such training as is required is presented and so that it is learned in an appropriate amount of time. For example, are there rules to be learned, compare-and-contrast exercises required, models to be built or demonstrations to be performed, problems to be defined and solved? How do you, as a manager, see the instructor's role—as a coach, a facilitator, an example, a leader, a coordinator, an information resource, a monitor?

Your third task as a manager is to get the right training to the right people so that the resources it uses up are an investment in productivity.

Productivity

Employees, managers, executives, officers, owners, and customers of a company all benefit from a smoothly running, well-tuned, productive business. In simplest terms, in such a business the outputs exceed the inputs:

$$\text{Productivity} = \frac{\text{output}}{\text{input}}.$$

Your Productivity

Your productivity as a manager will be measured by how you handle your responsibilities as a supervisor of employees and as an operations head. The dual nature of management, supervisory as well as operational, requires that you continually strive to optimize the corporate resources of material, information, and people to maintain a favorable balance of outputs over inputs.

Training can help you deal with both your supervisory and operational responsibilities. The following ideas can get you started:

Productivity as a Supervisor

Think of the many facets of your job as a supervisor. If you can't remember what they are because they've become intertwined with your operations job, take a look at your job description. Chances are you'll find that the personnel tasks of your job include these basics: hiring and terminating employees, maintaining attendance, ensuring communications, and representing corporate policies and disseminating corporate procedures within the group of employees who report to you. Your worth as a supervisor depends on how effectively you expend your resources to accomplish these tasks.

Your productivity as related to your supervisory responsibilities could be adversely affected by an excessive input balance or a reduced output balance in the tasks of supervision. For example, your group might have high turnover, incidence of white-collar crime, legal suits over unfair terminations, poor attendance, repeated evidence of communication breakdowns, or misunderstandings and errors in carrying out corporate policies and procedures. These inputs are quantified and measured in units of time, dollars, and frequency of errors.

Training that is related to any of these typical tasks can help you increase output and reduce those excessive input numbers, bringing your productivity formula into better balance. For example, be sure your employees know the rules about attendance, have the proper forms at hand to document attendance and know how to fill them out, know about probationary periods, know about employment rights and responsibilities, receive adequate orientation about the company, and are kept informed on a regular basis regarding important business matters.

Think of the kind of training you might have to offer: Is it knowledge training, attitude training, or skill training? Your "inputs" expenditures will remain in better balance when you plan for the right kind of training. Inputs are expended unnecessarily when you try to train all people in all things. As you choose only the training methods and content that are appropriate to your employees' needs, you expend fewer input resources (time, money, materials) and become more productive. As your employees use up fewer input resources back on the job because they know more about what's expected of them, you also become more productive as a supervisor.

Productivity as an Operations Head

Think, too, of your responsibilities as the head of your particular operation. Think of how you are measured on the way in which the tasks of operations are done. Think of how better training for your employees in these operational tasks might result in a reduced expenditure of input resources or an increased output. Here are some of the typical areas to investigate when you are trying to become a more productive operations manager: relevance and timeliness of job information, maintenance and calibration of equipment, frequency of service, quantity of inventory, amount of good versus bad product made, quality of service, and quality of product.

Your productivity as an operations head will be adversely affected when any of these operational areas indicates an excess of resource expenditure. The excess can take the form of too much information, too many programs, irrelevant memos, off-target reports, systems and books that are not needed, information overload leading to decision paralysis, time spent fixing equipment that doesn't work, too much, inappropriate, or the wrong type of service, excessive inventory, product recalls, and customer complaints.

Training targeted at any of these problem areas before they become problems can help prevent the input/output imbalance. Your trained employees will use up fewer resources and give your operation a better chance of achieving greater output, as indicated by such measures as repeat business, fewer product returns, less scrap, more good units produced per employee, fewer customer service complaints, and increased sales per employee.

Targeted training to help employees do their jobs better is the kind of training that teaches procedures, focuses on attitudes, and develops skills that will make operations safer, more effective, and more interesting. By thinking of your job as a manager with two distinct types of responsibilities, supervision and operations, you'll be able to make better decisions about who needs what kind of training to improve productivity.

Productive Employees

More productive employees can be found everywhere. They inhabit all departments and all levels, work in groups or alone, and interact with suppliers, distributors, customers, and board members. The productive employee consistently tries to get more units of output per unit of input—for example, per labor hour, per machine, per pound of raw material, per line of code.

Playing on the Team

Productive work groups have certain characteristics: Their members focus on problems, how to solve them and how to prevent them; they see problems as opportunities to improve; they share information and intuition; they design quality into processes as they go along and into products during the early stages of product design and development; they monitor and check each other's work. Group members quantify, measure, test, and communicate.

Managers can help productive work groups continually improve productivity by providing leadership that demonstrates a commitment to quality at every level of product, process, and service. Managers can help employees by providing training in testing methodology, in measurement options, in systems analysis, in monitoring and evaluation strategies, in giving and receiving feedback, and in standards of the business. Managers can search for or create seminars, courses, and training conferences in the techniques of interaction that lead to increased output during teamwork on the job.

Doing It Solo

The productive individual employee will also be a problem solver, analyst, and communicator. The productive individual will also continually monitor herself against corporate standards and against her own personal code of behavior. She will strive to contain all costs, understand the elements of pricing, and have a sense of balance regarding labor expenditures as well as capital expenditures. She will also focus on accuracy, clarity, completeness, doing it right the first time, being consistent, being on time, being dependable, and being open to continual corrective improvement.

Managers can provide individuals with many tools to help them increase the quality and quantity of their output. Training in standards and measurements is critical, as is providing opportunities for employees to see the results of their work. A commitment to quality, demonstrated by visible and consistent implementation of quality policies and recognition of quality successes, is also an important management responsibility that can inspire individuals to continually improve productivity.

Productivity and Quality

Productivity ratios are related to quality ratios. Productivity improvement involves defining and quantifying factors that enhance and magnify the inputs to increase the quality of outputs. Productivity improvement also involves reducing the inputs, that is, reducing the work expended or the resources expended, so that the outputs outweigh the inputs in terms of value to the organization in terms of quality.

Training is perhaps the most direct way of improving work and of ensuring the wise use of resources. Good training can be expected to significantly improve both productivity and quality.

Quality ratios are generally expressed as some degree of approximation or conformance to standards. They are sometimes defined as how ready a process is for application, or how ready a product is for the marketplace. If you think of the development and deployment of the human resources in a corporation as a strategic tool, you can imagine that how well those resources are trained in the essential knowledge, attitudes, and skills of the business will indeed affect your business strategy. Training and retraining will help you in your efforts to conform to standards.

Training as a factor contributing to a company's assets, customer satisfaction, high standards, reputation, and increased output makes it a valuable tool for building a better business. Good training pays off.

Motivation

No matter what your point of view is on how to motivate people, you probably believe that motivated people contribute the most to an organization. Chances are that the most productive organizations are well-tuned in terms of the way in which employees fit their jobs. Motivated employees work for a purpose, know what the results will be, believe that their contributions are valued, and appear to have in mind the big picture of how their work helps carry out the mission of the company.

Big-Time Success

Training contributes to motivating employees first through the careful analysis phase that you as a manager go through when you begin planning a training experience for a particular employee or group of employees. Training planning forces you to think seriously about what a specific person needs to know in order to do a job better. Training planning forces you to really understand—to precisely define, to prioritize—what your organization is supposed to do and how your employees, your organization, and you as a manager are measured. It also forces you to think clearly about your budget and the prudent use of company resources. Training contributes to motivation by focusing both on what's best for the individual and on what's best for the company. Big-time success happens when work output and quality improve and resources are reinvested in corporate growth.

Training also contributes in a major way to the quality and effectiveness of each process involved in doing a job. Good training is designed around the specific tasks of a specific job. Its success is measured by how well a person can do those specific tasks after training. Well-trained employees will be capable of doing better-quality work, and for many people the personal satisfaction of doing a good job is a powerful motivator to do an even better job in the future.

When you go though the exercise of determining who needs what training, you often uncover flaws or errors in existing processes. Although it takes time to do the analysis right, it's time well invested to be sure that the training is designed for the correct process. Training's credibility and your credibility as a manager increase when "broken" processes are fixed before training begins and the training is right on target. The right training motivates employees to stick with it until they can master what's being taught.

Training is a proven process for accomplishing behavioral change, a way to "get there from here." The wise manager will also see its application to motivating employees.

Small-Time Success

Training improves the competencies of human resources and the usefulness of machinery in many small ways. A good manager will recognize that lots of small successes in improved skills, attitudes, and knowledge will accumulate over time into continual improvement. A good rule of thumb is to think small when you make training decisions. Offering many, right-on-target training opportunities, each taking up only a short time, is far better in most instances than sending employees away for a week of training. Recognizing and rewarding small successes can be a powerful way of building motivation to keep doing a better job.

There are incentives other than the intrinsic motivation of doing high-quality work that keep people on the job. People work for money, to fulfill family responsibilities, to receive approval, or because they fear unemployment. Some people work only enough to get by, and those who work for these reasons also need the right kinds of motivation to keep them on the job.

Training can help here too. Training that addresses standards of acceptable performance, clarifies the procedures of a job, instructs workers in the skills required and the new tools available for doing a job, encourages communication, and provides feedback can all help keep workers on the job. Training is a powerful tool for maintaining work as well as for improving work.

Training's Hidden Power

A frequent spin-off benefit of training is improved communications. Because of the nature of training interactions, training becomes a vehicle for learning and practicing all sorts of good communication skills. Training's hidden power is improved communications that benefit both the big-time successes of the highly productive employee and the small-time successes of those whose work is simply being maintained in a viable way.

Trainees share a common bond of "needing to know." They all come to the training experience as learners and as individuals who are more or less willing to risk being exposed as workers who don't know. Good training supports individuals who ask questions, who need clarification, and who volunteer information to move lessons forward. Giving support and sharing information help create a climate for improved communications at a fundamental human relations level. Employees who have more finely tuned communications skills function better in committees, task forces, and work groups of all sizes. Training works through communications to support employees in many aspects of work.

In classrooms of trainees, good instruction will encourage interaction among trainees and will use the diverse job experiences of the individuals present to make instruction more interesting. Employees who get the idea that their opinions about and experiences at work are valued by others will be more receptive to elaboration, creative thinking, and applying feedback. Interactive communications during training help to motivate employees.

The trick for managers is to catch the receptive employee as soon after training as possible in order to capitalize on training's hidden communication power. Classrooms can be very effective laboratories for communication in addition to being places for learning. The "training system" of analysis, development, and evaluation uses feedback as a standard practice to improve courses. Trainees are typically exercised in the use of feedback, and can be expected to be more aware communicators as a result of having been in a course that encourages giving and receiving feedback in both oral and written forms.

A wide dissemination of information typically takes place during the setup operation prior to training. The occasion of training often requires widespread distribution of brochures, electronic messages, and telephone calls. During this time, communication channels are often working well, and new channels of communication become open. The wise manager will look for opportunities to enhance corporate communications as training is getting off the ground. Good communication can contribute to motivating employees to enhance and maintain good work.

What People Need to Learn

People at work require management, support, and opportunities in order to increase productivity. Managers can begin to structure the development of their human resources by thinking about what their employees need in the three essential areas of knowledge, attitudes, and skills. Training opportunities can be found here:

KNOWLEDGE

• *Information about the customer's business:* How the customer uses our product, our services, our information; what the customer's standards are and how we are helping the customer meet those standards; how our products and services help the customer grow; what we contribute to the customer's profitability.

• *Standards:* Clear statements of our standards of excellence and achievement; clear descriptions of our measurements for product quality, service quality, and personal effectiveness; clear statements of the evaluation criteria used in the performance review.

• *Professionalism:* Knowledge of what constitutes professional behavior in this company; what the accepted practices are regarding communications with supervisors, peers, subordinates, customers, suppliers; what the dress codes are; what constitutes acceptable social behavior at work.

• *Job information:* What is the full range of job information I am expected to have or to acquire? To whom should I go for the information I lack? What is my responsibility for getting the information I need, and what can I expect the company or my manager to provide? What books and library resources am I expected to use? What is the procedure to follow if I try but cannot find the information I need to do my job properly? What are the specific requirements of my job?

• *Company information:* What is the business of this company? What is its financial status? Who are the company's officers and operating executives? Where do I fit in the organization chart? What other jobs could I qualify for and what are my options for growth or broadening within this company? What avenues do I take to make knowledge of the company work for me?

Attitudes

• *Fairness:* Need to be treated fairly in relationship to the way other employees are treated and in relationship to the goals and standards of my particular job. I need to treat others fairly also.

• *Openness:* Need to be dealt with openly, directly, and honestly in order to do the best job I am capable of doing. I need to deal openly with others too.

• *Respect:* Need to be accorded respect for who I am as a person, as a worker in this particular job, and as a fellow contributor to the well-being of this company. I need to respect others as they respect me.

• *Compassion:* Need to receive the compassion and empathy of supervisors and peers at times of personal adversity and at times of difficulty and stress created by the job. I need to treat others with compassion too.

• *Support:* Support for my work from clerical, technical, and professional staff whose jobs are interrelated with my job. I expect to be able to give support to those who require it from me.

• *Management:* Expectation that management will facilitate my work.

• *Leadership:* Expectation that management will act assertively and proactively to enable me to strengthen the company. I expect to be able to develop leadership skills and attitudes of my own.

• *Responsiveness:* Expectation that management will respond to my efforts and concern for the good of the company by providing timely and useful feedback and the resources I need to do my job.

SKILLS

• *Procedures:* Step-by-step instructions on how to do a task or a whole job related to any of the many functions of the company.

• *Models:* Designs or models that accurately represent the real thing; graphic representations that make my job clearer and help me to do it better.

• *Criteria:* Standards of performance that tell me exactly what I need to do and what constitutes acceptable work; criteria that tell me what is the extra measure that defines quality; specific measures of quantity such as how many, what level, how long, what percent; standards of performance that are directly related to skills I have or can acquire in order to do my job.

• *Tools that work:* Tools that work the way they should work so that I can do my job efficiently; tools that have been maintained and are in good condition; tools that are necessary for me to do my job—the right tools.

• *Tools and work environment that are safe:* Tools and a work environment free from electronic, chemical, physical, and psychological hazards that would impede the use of my skills or impair my health.

• *Requirements:* Skill requirements that are current, updated, and relevant to actual work; requirements that are realistic; skills that are attainable; opportunities for acquiring new skills and upgrading existing skills.

The tool of training can help you to develop your human resources in a structured way by addressing your employees' needs for knowledge, attitudes, and skills that lead to continually improving productivity. Appropriate and timely training is an important management responsibility that can have a quick and substantial payoff. Thinking about the specific purpose of training in the areas of knowledge, attitudes, and skills will start you off on the right track.

Basic Guidelines

There are a few basic guidelines for managing training, for making practical sense out of all the ideas presented earlier in this chapter.

Building on Experience

The first is to design the training so that it will be practical, hands-on, and directly relevant.

1. *Get the trainee involved.* Maneuver the trainee into the position of having to ask many questions; reinforce the trainee's insights with compliments and positive feedback; get the trainee to rethink an incorrect response by leading him step by logical step through a diagnostic exercise; encourage trainees to think aloud and to solve their own problems, perhaps by starting with the solution and working backwards; avoid "telling" adult learners what to do.

Use a hands-on approach whenever you can. Let trainees try out new equipment, make mistakes, and learn in their own time. Realize that each person's experience base regarding the new equipment will vary and that some adult learners will learn faster than others because of that difference. Pair up an experienced learner with one not so experienced so that points of view can be shared and the more experienced person can help the less experienced person. Ask a student who obviously "got it" to demonstrate the correct operation for other trainees, and point out the critical points of learning as your student takes over the role of teacher during the demonstration. Think of yourself as a facilitator of learning, not as a geyser gushing forth all knowledge. Respect your adult students as individuals who already possess great amounts of knowledge and skills.

Encourage your students to imagine how and when they will use what you are teaching them during this training. At several points during training, ask them how the training will be helpful on their jobs, as a reality check on the relevance of the course. Be flexible enough to modify your training plan so that the course or training exercise continues to be exactly to the point and useful for these particular trainees.

2. *Group trainees according to their interests.* Generally speaking, people at work who go to class would rather be back at work than in the classroom. They view training as something other than their real jobs. In order to make training as interesting as possible, keep it small and simple; that is, design lessons around two or three objectives that a small number of people can relate to. It's better to thoroughly serve a handful of people than to superficially reach large numbers of trainees in a mistaken attempt at efficiency. Training will run more smoothly and trainees will learn more if training is very focused. Workers in class will rebel at having to deal with information or skills that they see as irrelevant to their jobs.

Consider organizing a large class around specific interest areas. Examples might be product introduction workshops; account maintenance workshops for specific products in sales training; or workshops on how to create tables and charts, how to import graphic files, or how to use various type sizes and styles in desktop publishing. Understand that workers in class want training to be as much like their jobs as possible. Encourage them to talk about solutions to specific problems they face on the job. Trainees are seldom in training for the intrinsic value of the content. They are there because they need or want to learn how to do their work better.

3. *Vary your style of instructing.* Realize that people over age 20 know pretty well the learning approaches that work best for them: memorizing a set of rules and systematically applying them to new situations; having a "cheat sheet" or job aid always handy so that memorizing isn't necessary; rehearsing or practicing over and over again; smelling, feeling vibrations, observing the flow of a process; listening to an audiotape while driving to work; having videotape at home to play and replay as needed; having a periodic formal dialogue with a mentor or more ad-

vanced colleague; meeting informally with friends who share their job experiences; reporting back to an authority figure who certifies mastery or who gives grades; reading books, highlighting sections, and making notes in the margins for review later on; imagining solutions or inventing new applications; going through case studies; building a model; playing computer games; or teaching others.

The ways of learning are many and complex. The effective instructor will try to tap into the preferred learning style of each student and present the training so that it fits with that style.

Overcoming the Aversion to Training

The basic reason that both managers and employees have an aversion to training is that both tend to see training as costing too much. The real work of a company is almost always thought of as something other than training. This means that neither the boss nor the subordinate feels very good about the time that is taken up during training.

Countering the perception that training costs too much is a tricky buisiness. The best way to convince all persons concerned that training really pays is for the training to directly address areas that have an impact on a company's profit. The training experience has to be so precisely in tune with the target trainee group or individual and the company's basic reasons for being in business that it doesn't take too much time. Training time has to be perceived as time that will add value to work, as a value-added function.

The first order of business, then, is to design or purchase training that is directly relevant to a business purpose and that affects the bottom line. Try very hard to avoid the temptation to go for convenience training—that is, training that fits conveniently into an open time slot, or seems to have the potential for reaching a mass audience all at once, or training that goes from page 1 through page 52 whether or not the content is relevant. Streamline your training; make it spare; don't waste time. Do training for the right reasons and you will quickly cure your own and your employees' aversions to training.

There are also aversions to training at the individual psychological level. The wise manager will tune into these characteristics of adult learners and take appropriate action to prevent negative results.

Some of these individual aversions relate to:

• *Failure*. Adult learners often fear failure. Therefore, be careful not to set up unrealistic norms; give plenty of positive feedback; reinforce successes during learning; refer to known successes on the job; provide space for trainees to fail in private.

• *Incompetence*. Adult learners don't like to look silly or incompetent in front of their peers. Take steps early in training to make each trainee feel comfortable. Be sure each trainee can articulate a personal goal for the training experience. Encourage trainees to measure their success during training by how close they come to the personal goals they have set. Be sure all trainees know that each learner's situation is slightly different from that of others. Don't set up "norms" that force a certain percentage of students to be classified in the incompetent bottom or tail end of the normal curve. Always keep lines of communication open so that each person knows that it's okay to make mistakes and to ask plenty of questions.

• *Labeling*. Adult learners don't like to be labeled or put into contrived groupings. Adults are individual learners. Don't make the mistake of pitching your training to an imaginary typical student. Don't make the mistake of assuming that this is a slow group or a lazy group, or a group of "moles" or geniuses. Be careful not to stereotype individuals or groups of trainees. There probably is not a "typical" student among your trainees. Make your training design flexible enough to accommodate a variety of job interests and individual styles. Design your training for individuals; and if those individuals happen to come together in a class, be sure you treat them as individual competent human beings, not as a classroom full of "types." Interact with individuals during training, always listening, encouraging, guiding, giving and seeking feedback.

Avoiding the Resource Drain

The bottom line, then, in the management of human resources is to avoid the resource drain of time, money, personnel, and work expended on tasks that don't add value. Said another way, the manager's job is to plan for and implement the expenditure of resources so that it becomes a factor for productivity, profit, growth, and development. Managers who choose training as an avenue for growth need to be aware of ways of planning for it and of implementing it that avoid the resource drain. Managers need to make training quick and effective. The following guidelines will start you in the right direction:

1. *Build in quality from the beginning.* Don't teach bad procedures: Fix them before beginning training design. Don't go the next step in trainee identification, program purchase, or course design until you've checked your decisions with several different kinds of people who have a stake in the results of every stage of the training you propose.

2. *Design small.* Design small sections of training around specific objectives for specific learners. Trying to be all things to all people will result in spending too much time in development and will diminish the impact of the delivery of training.

3. *Think creatively.* Save time by using the most appropriate delivery approach. Don't automatically think a course in a classroom is the best way. Be creative in your thinking of delivery methods: Consider charts, posters, videotapes, structured discussion groups, demonstrations.

4. *Shop around.* You may want to purchase outside training services and products. A word of caution: Don't be fooled by slick promotion or persistent salespersons. Go through a careful analysis process so that you can articulate accurately what you want. Be sure your potential service provider can meet your needs. Watch out for bells and whistles.

5. *Preview and customize.* Consider customizing a generic commercial product, for example, a videotape. Don't buy a training product without seeing it first—all of it. Be sure that the product isn't padded with irrelevant material, and be sure that

there are logical interruption points that allow you to insert your own information or to elaborate on what has been shown. Irrelevant material makes trainees angry and wastes resources.

6. *Provide equal opportunity.* Provide equal opportunity to a diverse trainee population. Realize that training is often viewed as an employment opportunity, as a precursor to promotion or a raise, and can be a factor in litigation by an individual against a corporation. Build in factors that guarantee equal opportunity in training—equal opportunity to get into training, and equal opportunity to succeed during and as a result of training. Provide the right training for the right people and you won't have any trouble. You'll always have a better chance of maximizing your human resources by paying attention to equal opportunity.

In Brief

In brief then, there are some key steps you ought to take to make training work for you. The following checklist will help you to plan for and to implement the kind of training that makes your employees more productive.

MANAGER'S CHECKLIST 1

How Training Makes Employees More Productive

_____   1. Convince the doubters by proving that good training pays off.

_____   2. Execute your responsibilities regarding training in the two major areas of supervision and operations.

_____   3. Design and deliver training around job experience.

_____   4. Design training for individual adults.

_____   5. Measure training's contribution to corporate growth by its effect on quality and productivity.

    6. Organize training needs into three areas: the need for new knowledge; the need for changed attitudes; and the need for improved skills.

    7. State the goals of training in terms of expected changes in behavior.

    8. Watch for a spinoff benefit in the communications area.

    9. Choose training that is spare and to the point; make training contribute to increased outputs and better invested inputs of your business.

    10. Tie training success to your company's formulas for quality and productivity.

    11. Exempt no employee group or level from the need for training.

    12. Use training to help motivate employees.

CHAPTER 2

How to Train Employees One-to-One

Part of your job as a manager is to get an employee on the job quickly and to get new work going as soon as possible. To do this often means that you become a one-to-one trainer.

This chapter gives you concrete guidance on how to carry out your responsibility to an individual employee when he needs training. It suggests proven ways in which you can function as a trainer with little or no preparation. The chapter gives you some guidance on spotting those situations where you might be most effective as a trainer, and shows you what you must do in order to design and deliver training in a way that helps your trainee to learn. You'll see what's involved in a lesson, get some time-saving tips for scheduling training, and have a chance to look at sample lessons for some typical one-to-one training.

Situations That Suggest One-to-One Training

Because you have the vision and can provide the leadership, you are the one most likely to succeed at delivering the training.

Your focus, as a manager, on profitability and productivity makes you the ideal candidate to design and deliver training to a single employee at a critical juncture when new knowledge or skills are required. You know what needs to be learned, you know what isn't necessary to learn, and you know what that individual is like at work. You know basically what it will take for that employee's work output to become an asset to your business.

Training one-to-one is a highly effective, money-saving, time-saving way of teaching an employee. This is because you start from the base of knowing quite a bit about the trainee before you begin training, and both you and the trainee are very focused on the goal of training. These two advantages allow you as a manager to step into your role as trainer without needing any introduction or any credibility-building. As the trainee's manager, you can conveniently schedule the training time so that it doesn't negatively affect work output. Your trainee is always close at hand, working for the goals you're working for. Distractions from other work or other trainees are simply not there.

These are some typical situations where one-to-one training is indicated:

For Existing Employees

- A performance review points out a specific task or business function at which the employee must do better in order to maintain an acceptable performance rating.
- The employee has just returned to your department from a rotational assignment of several months and needs to catch up on the changes that have been made since she left.
- The employee has just returned from a medical disability leave. You want to be sure exactly what kind of work he can do now.
- Your boss wants to learn how to use her new personal computer.
- The work of a highly specialized technical employee is affected by the direction being taken by the company subsequent to its merger with another corporation. You have to

interpret the new business direction to this employee and help her to change approach.

- Research has indicated that radiation levels may be unsafe and eye fatigue excessive for certain kinds of workers who work long stretches at a video display terminal. You have two such workers. Each needs individual attention to see if there is a problem and, if there is, to correct it and find out how work can be performed at the same level without personal harm.
- Computerized controls have replaced mechanical controls. Because each employee is responsible for a different set of controllers, each needs one-to-one training on how to do the same job with the new controls.
- An employee who has just had a job change but who still reports to you needs to know what's involved in the new assignment. An example is a secretary who now has to perform customer service functions.

FOR NEW EMPLOYEES

- A new employee reports to the jobsite after having gone through a personnel orientation in the central personnel office.
- You have agreed to accept an employee for a "career broadening" rotational assignment in your department.
- A summer intern reports for work.
- You have provided temporary office space to a corporate attorney gathering data for a case he is working on. Although not directly reporting to you, he will be using your building services and your secretary during his stay.
- You have been promoted and are moving out of state. Your successor will have two days to spend with you before you leave.

FOR NEW WORK

- You have chosen one of your employees as manager of a new project and must bring him up to speed regarding the new work.
- You will become the manager of an acquired company's

previous manager of the department similar to yours. You want to be sure she knows how you will do business as an expanded department.

- You have decided to purchase an inventory control system from a business service agency. The person you are moving into the job of inventory control manager needs to know what it's all about.

- You are adding computerized graphics production capabilities to your word processing and spreadsheet applications. The employee in charge of graphics production needs to know about your commitments to upper management and what the new parameters and procedures of his job now are.

Giving Training Your Best Shot

Think of your role as trainer as an extension of your role as leader. That is, a good trainer leads a trainee to right answers, and facilitates the thought and actions of that trainee by steering, suggesting, showing, guiding. Your best shot at delivering training will come when you see yourself as a facilitative leader who points the way and walks beside the trainee.

The following ideas can help you to see why this kind of one-to-one training has an excellent chance of achieving results, saving money, and saving time.

Achieving Results

Good results in training are generally measured in two basic ways—by the degree to which a trainee seems to understand the material during the time spent with you in the training session itself, and by how quickly the new information or skill can be implemented on the job. There are elements of loading your brain with content, your fingers with skills, and your soul with confidence when you measure the results of training.

When you design training around specific areas of content, think very specifically about what it takes to master that area. This kind of thinking is necessary whether it's 20 things you need to share with your successor who'll be with you for two days or whether it's how to load software and print color graphics using the new electronic workstation.

Your successor must have certain levels of knowledge or certain amounts of information. Your graphics person needs to know the best way to perform the tasks you outline to make the new software and hardware work. Be clear in your own mind what these standards for mastery are for each employee you have to train. Is 85 percent accuracy good enough during training, or do you require 100 percent? Will you need to spend some after-hours time with your successor if he doesn't quite master the information you present? Know what your acceptable levels of achievement are, let the trainee know them, and work at training until those levels are attained.

List the major topics of training on a chart with room beside each topic to indicate the mastery level that is appropriate. Give the trainee many chances during training to show you that he is moving toward that mastery level. Engage often in dialogue with the trainee, frequently ask him questions, and let the trainee demonstrate a new skill to show you he understands and can use that new skill. Lead him to success. Applaud and reinforce small successful steps along the way.

Saving Money

Training one-to-one is a good technique for saving training money because you have a built-in expert, yourself. You do not need to pay for outside course development or personnel. You also don't need to give the trainee lots of training materials to use later after the instructor has disappeared. You are the instructor, and you're not likely to disappear after the training session. You'll probably be around in case the trainee needs help later. When you do training one-to-one, you tend to save development costs.

You also save hotel and travel expenses called for when you send an employee to an outside training program, and you save the employee's salary that is typically lost by his being off the job. One-to-one training can be done on the job with very little impact on salary loss during training.

Saving Time

One-to-one training is a time saver because the communication line is typically short between you and your trainee prior to, during, and after training. You can dispense with catalogs, announcements, registration campaigns, and the elaborate assembly of training manuals, slides, and audiovisual equipment.

The trainee in a one-to-one training situation is already focused on the topic or topics of training because of the requirements of his unique job situation. You don't have to waste time figuring out what it is that this person needs to know—you already know that, and so does he. The one-to-one trainee has a strong interest in doing well when you are the trainer; you seldom have to whip up motivation. In one-to-one training, there's no ganging up on the boring instructor—no clandestine coffee break agreements to leave early, no opportunity for the trainee to show up late because of wanting to make just one more phone call before coming to class. When you are the trainer, training becomes the trainee's number one priority. The time given to one-to-one training is almost always totally useful learning time.

How to Prepare Mentally for One-to-One Training

When you step out of your role as manager and into your role as trainer, the most important thing to think about is the objectives you have for this particular learner. This particular individual needs to know things that probably no one else needs to know. Think about this person's productivity in a very narrow way. What does she have to change about the way she operates, or what totally new things does she need to know? Think about these changes as small steps.

Think about training this person in knowledge, attitudes, and skills to help her perform at her best. "Necessary" and "sufficient'' are the key words—*only* what's necessary, and *all* that's sufficient. Remember that you are trying to improve work output by investing in work input.

The Learner's Personal Goals

Before beginning your training session(s), sit down with your trainee to talk about how he conceives the goals of training. Keep your discussion focused on the specific goals of training, not life or career goals. You know what you want your employee to be capable of doing, and you have a fairly good idea of what it will take for him to get there. But in this conversation, let the employee tell you what he hopes to learn. Stay focused on the knowledge, attitudes, and skills pertaining to the employee's job.

Make it clear to the employee that this is not a performance review discussion. It is simply an exercise in sharpening the tool of training. Get the employee to think of training as a specific and well-defined activity of business, just as one would think of filling out paperwork or preparing a budget or deploying a trucking fleet as specific and well-defined areas of the business. As in these activities, in training, too, you have to think in terms of step-by-step procedures and employing specific techniques or principles to get the job done in the best way.

Get the trainee to be specific about training goals so that you can match up what he feels he needs to know with what you think he needs to know. You'll be surprised in two ways. First, most trainees will be in agreement with you as to the desired outcome; and second, most trainees will be able to tell you specifically where their weaknesses are. This can come as a surprise because at work employees often hide or compensate for their deficiencies. They get others to cover for them, or they make so much work for themselves in other areas that they simply don't do those tasks in which they lack ability or confidence. When pressed to be specific about knowledge and skill deficiencies in the context of this training activity, most employees will be able to steer you right to their weak areas.

Use the brief outline presented in Figure 1 to guide your

Figure 1.   Outline of learner's personal training goals.

---

1. **Content.** What specific areas of your job are unclear? What seems to be missing? What looks like a real challenge? What is too hard? What are you afraid to tackle? What is unnecessary? [*Phrase the questions so that the learner cannot answer yes or no: You want information, not a cover-up.*]

   _____

   _____

   _____

   _____

2. **Goals.** Where do you think you should be regarding each of the content areas listed in item 1? What are your own personal goals regarding each aspect of the job?

   _____

   _____

   _____

   _____

3. **Action.** What do you have to do or learn to achieve your personal goals? [*It is critical here that the trainee think of actions related to each individual goal.*]

   _____

   _____

   _____

   _____

---

discussion. Or, you might prefer to give these points to your trainee a day or two before your discussion so that he can come to the discussion prepared. Listen during the discussion. Don't talk too much. Use all of your supervisory skills of "active listening." View this exercise as a fact-finding mission. Be prepared for surprises, and stay focused on training needs. Don't let the discussion deteriorate into a confession or cover-your-tail meeting. Summarize the discussion by writing down what the trainee said about his special training needs. Show what you have written to the trainee before he leaves the discussion meeting. Keep any written material he might have prepared for you. Smile.

Use the outline given in Figure 1 for trainees to identify their personal training goals. Either give it to the trainee to fill out, or use the three discussion points during a face-to-face meeting with the trainee.

Understanding Individual Learning Styles

Learning is a complicated process that involves a person's adaptation to change through the successful use of techniques that work. One's personal learning style involves a practical choice from among many options. Learning style is related to an individual's values, family influences, personality, and past successes.

The important thing for a one-to-one trainer to remember is that each individual trainee probably exhibits an imbalanced combination of learning style preferences. One trainee may learn some things better by observing, other things by experimenting. Some trainees need lots of graphic clues and relate to patterns, models, and drawings. Some trainees require a serene environment; others need the activity of the daily work environment in order to focus. Some trainees learn by shutting out everything else around them to make room for the new learning; others absorb everything around them, synthesize, and prioritize factors of influence on the new learning. The list of ways in which people learn is very long.

Most trainees have an idea of what their preferred learning

style is. They may even be able to tell you in what ways they'd like to improve their learning capacity or expand their use of different learning styles.

For example, a trainee may not be so good at imagining what a product might look like if a new process were applied in creating that product. Your training in this instance might be focused in part on helping her to develop an ability to look beyond a current situation, to learn to collect more information before acting, and to listen with a more open mind to "blue-sky" thinkers. You might have to assure her that a little day-dreaming is okay at work.

Or, your trainee may not know how to organize information. Her style of learning may not place a value on organization; she may even believe that organization is the refuge of weak minds. In addition to moderating such a value judgment, you'll have to teach this employee some specific skills regarding organizing information. As you do one-to-one training, be prepared to identify your trainee's learning style and to tailor your teaching to meet or supplement that style.

Sometimes, however, you'll find that it's just not worth trying to change a person's values when they are deeply ingrained. In that case, it might be better to change the employee's job assignment to one that is not heavily dependent on organization, and to train the person for tasks that don't require functioning within a style that's not a preferred learning style. Remember, training is an investment in the human resources you have. Don't use up your time and energy or your trainee's time and energy in an unproductive way. Do as much as you can to tailor that training experience to the specific person you're dealing with.

If you or your trainee can't verbalize anything about learning style, you can listen for clues in the way the trainee talks to you about her job. For instance, does she use such words as "I feel" or "I think"? "I question whether" or "I have proved"? "My gut reaction is" or "That's the logical conclusion"? "The truth is" or "That's not practical"? "I see" or "I hear"?

As a one-to-one trainer, sensitize yourself to the clues your employee gives you regarding how she does the job so that you have a good starting place for creating an effective training experience that is truly an investment in her. Don't waste your time expounding on all the newest theories about work if she consistently uses words like "I see." She probably needs concrete evidence so that she can see what's happening.

If you know an employee learns, works, and succeeds by listening to the way a motor hums or by feeling the vibrations of the machinery for which he is responsible, don't attempt to teach new machines by reviewing the operations manual step by step. Start the machine, and let him hear and feel how it works. If you back into the essential content (the operations manual) through his preferred learning style, your training will be much more effective and efficient.

Basic Instructional Strategies

There are some basic instructional strategies that seem to work with most trainees. These ways of presenting instruction are more related to the psychology of learning than they are to any particular learning style. As a one-to-one trainer, build these instructional techniques into your teaching:

1. *Present the big picture.* Describe the way the job should be done; describe the effect of the new equipment; describe the organization into which this work will fit; describe the benefits of doing something differently; describe what it should look like if it works properly. Most employees like to make a contribution to the total work. Describe that total work so that your trainee can see his role in it.

2. *Review the requirements.* Be sure that the trainee understands what the new task or situation requires. Take the time to clarify, explain, prioritize, and elaborate where she seems to lack information. Most people like to know where they're going and what the weather's like there before they start out on the trip.

3. *Fill in the gaps.* Provide the trainee with the prerequisite information he lacks. Point him in the direction of people or documents that will be of service in the areas of information

deficiency. Limit this gap-filling activity to those items that will be specifically helpful to him in this specific training. For example you might need to provide your successor with an up-to-the-minute organization chart that includes impending transfers and retirements; to provide the VDT user with copies of current federal and state legislation; or to arrange with another operator for your trainee to shadow her during a typical startup and shutdown operation that must be mastered before he can be trained on flowthrough procedures.

4. *Take the trainee from where he currently is.* After you've given the trainee an opportunity to catch up on a few critical prerequisite items, begin your training from where he is in terms of understanding of the job. Build on his experience; ease into skill-building gradually. Don't overwhelm your employee with your superior knowledge or skill; show him that you appreciate where he is at the moment and that you do understand his work.

There's a certain mind-set in teaching adults that helps the teaching/learning process: Every adult at work is a competent human being in some way and has been a successful learner. As a one-to-one trainer, you must get across the idea that you respect this person's way of doing things and are aware of his successes. One-to-one training is intense and focused pretty much on that trainee alone. This mind-set can temper the intense scrutiny that most employees feel subjected to during training.

5. *Present your instruction in the form of a problem to be solved.* Give the trainee some cues on how to go about it, for instance by encouraging him to use his experience in solving other, perhaps similar, problems. Get the trainee to tell you the steps that were required to solve the problem. Give him feedback during his description of the problem-solving procedure.

6. *Demonstrate, or at least talk about, the desired outcome.* This goes along with presenting the big picture, but is a smaller part of it. If you are training someone to follow a new procedure, describe what the outcome of using that procedure will be. If you are training someone to operate a new machine, show her an example of a finished product made from that new machine or the documentation records from the work of a person using that new machine. Make the outcome of training real. If you are

training someone to make a chart or write an outline, use a flipchart or overhead transparency to show exactly what it should look like. Use her job data as sample data. Show that you know her standards and job specifications.

7. *Provide feedback and suggestions for correction.* Give the trainee praise when it's deserved at small steps all along the way. Also stop the trainee when he has done something wrong or just doesn't get it, and give him specific suggestions about what to do to correct the situation. Tell him how to prevent wrong action or wrong thinking. Be patient during both kinds of feedback so that he can internalize the actions and thinking that are necessary to do the job right. Approach the act of instructing as a series of very small steps, each of which involves feedback. Give clues.

8. *Plan for follow-up.* Build into your training some occasion for follow-up to see if the trainee is using the new skills and knowledge effectively on the job. Make it clear to the trainee when this will occur and what kind of monitoring or checking you intend to do. Better yet, get the trainee to tell you what he thinks will be the best kind of follow-up and when it should occur. Planning for follow-up helps keep your one-to-one training focused on real work, not work theory.

9. *Provide a crutch.* Even in a one-to-one training situation, trainees like to have a handout, paper item, or model to take back to the job or to take home for review. At the very least, provide your trainee with a content outline of the training, double-spaced or typed with large margins so that she can make personal notes on the outline. Providing a flowchart of a process, a job aid or card containing key operating instructions, or a copy of her personal goals for this training gives the trainee a frame of reference during the training and can jog her memory several months later. Because one-to-one training is more informal than classroom training, it may be perceived as a friendly encounter instead of a special business function. A handout of some sort helps formalize one-to-one training as well as provide the trainee with a learning crutch.

Making Training a Little Different From Working

It is important to make the training experience meaningful as training. It should therefore be set up to stand out from the everyday work experience while being directly related to it. The following four guidelines will help you.

1. *Make it job related.* Approximate the conditions of the job when you do one-to-one training. If you are training someone to use a new piece of equipment, be sure the new equipment is installed in a space similar to that in which it will be installed on the job. Part of a person's adaptation to new work is adaptation to dimensions such as the height of the installation, the elbow room around the new machine, and the interruptions to lines of vision. Training should include information about the techniques of adapting to this kind of work environment.

Be sure that the terminology you use in training is the same as that used on the job. If you are training someone to follow new procedures, be sure that you have a copy of the procedures manual readily available so the trainee can handle it and get used to finding information in it. Don't teach skills or procedures in isolation.

2. *Find a place where you can meet without interruption.* Try to give at least one hour of uninterrupted time to each one-to-one training session. Plan on up to two hours, but no more. Most instructors and trainees become fatigued after two hours of one-to-one training. Realize that during training your trainee will be giving undivided attention to you, and that kind of relationship is different from what you usually have with your employees. Be prepared psychologically to engage in this sort of focused and sustained meeting. Find a place where you will not be interrupted so that you and your trainee can get the most out of this special kind of time together, and where you can constantly interact with each other around the objectives of training. Uninterrupted space gives you time for proper feedback and a place to carry out demonstrations of the way things should be as a result of training.

3. *Make the space comfortable, clean, and uncluttered.* People should feel good about training, look upon it as an employment opportunity and as an opportunity for personal growth. Being chosen for training is often seen as an indication that the manager thinks the employee's work is valuable. Having you as the trainer can reinforce this sense of worth in your employee. Help to build the positive images about training by treating your trainee nicely during training. Make the training space comfortable, provide coffee, be sure the training materials are clean and the training space is cleared of trash and irrelevant clutter. A lunchroom table with stale cigarette butts in the ashtray and you with a few handwritten notes in your pocket do not provide the right learning environment.

4. *Prepare good, but minimal, learning aids and materials.* If you prepare any training materials for your trainee, such as charts, outlines, or instructions, be sure they are of good quality. Give as much attention to the quality of learning aids for one trainee as you would for a classroom full of students. In one-to-one training, it's the quantity that's different, that's all.

What to Do During a Lesson

A lesson can be thought of as a convenient boundary around a part of your instruction. Lesson designations are important because they give you, the instructor, a signal that you are coming to the end of a certain idea and need to get ready for presenting the next idea, and lessons are important to the learner because they represent a cohesive body of information. It's your job as an instructor to break up your period of instruction into lessons that can be taught and learned.

The 15-Minute Plan

A lesson plan for one-to-one instruction should cover about 15 minutes of learning time. That is, if you intend to do your training for one hour, you should develop four 15-minute lesson plans. Each one should be about one page long. These four pages become your instructor guide as you teach your trainee.

Make your lesson plan simple and easy for you to read at arm's length. This is because in one-to-one training, you will not be standing at a lectern or sitting at a desk. More likely, you will to be seated beside the trainee or moving around the room with the trainee as you teach. You need a piece of paper that is easy to read because it is not likely to remain in one place during instruction. In one-to-one training, you tend to toss your lesson plans here and there as you move from place to place. Be sure the writing is dark, clear, and big enough for you to see from a short distance if you need to.

What to Put Into a Lesson Plan

Your lesson plan tells you what you need to do to help the trainee learn something during this 15-minute period. It should contain brief lists rather than narrative passages. It should resemble an outline, such as the one shown in Figure 2. It should have wide margins so that you can make notes to yourself as you go along. Above all, it should serve you as you help your trainee to master something new.

These are the items to include in a one-page lesson plan:

- Title of the lesson
- Purpose of the lesson from the trainee's point of view
- Several specific behavioral objectives that can be achieved by the trainee during this 15-minute period
  - If your lesson is a lesson in learning new skills, also make a list of the tasks you will be teaching the trainee to do. You can use this list as a checklist, checking off tasks that were mastered as you go through the training session.
  - If your lesson is a lesson in learning new knowledge, it might help to coordinate a small feedback exercise with each item in your content section so that you have a way of judging whether or not your trainee got the message.
- A content outline of about four items
- A list of instructional aids or materials you'll need for this lesson

Figure 2.   Lesson plan format.

Lesson title: _____

Purpose of this lesson: _____

_____

Materials needed for this lesson:

_____   _____

_____   _____

Behavioral objectives for this lesson:

   1. _____

      _____

   2. _____

      _____

Content outline for this lesson:

   1. _____

      a. _____

      b. _____

   2. _____

      a. _____

      b. _____

   3. _____

      a. _____

      b. _____

Behavioral Objectives

There is no mystery about behavioral objectives. A behavioral objective is simply a short statement of what you expect the trainee to be able to do at the end of your attempt to teach him something. A behavioral objective is an action that the trainee can perform to show you that he has learned what you thought you taught. It is small and it is specific. Sample lessons at the end of this chapter show objectives in the context of a lesson.

Here are some examples:

- To identify
- To define
- To distinguish
- To sort
- To categorize
- To prioritize
- To compare
- To calculate
- To review
- To monitor
- To select
- To reduce
- To guide
- To load
- To alter

- To isolate
- To restructure
- To arrange
- To mark
- To place
- To find
- To assign
- To extract
- To transfer
- To connect
- To tally
- To straighten
- To convert
- . . . .

The list of actions by which your trainee might demonstrate that he can do what your training proposes to do is endless. When you write a lesson plan, think in terms of only a few behavioral objectives per 15-minute period. Only in this way, by thinking small, will you be able to know for sure that your trainee has learned.

Measurement

One of the key reasons why one-to-one training is very effective is that it presents an opportunity for measuring success. Because it is so personal and close, you have a chance to constantly interact with your trainee to test how he is doing. Small exercises every few minutes in which the trainee gives you feedback are excellent ways to test the trainee's new knowledge and skills.

You can do this in the following ways:

1. *Set a standard of achievement for each behavioral objective*. Examples are:

- with 90 percent accuracy
- of 10 items
- with zero defects
- with a maximum of three errors per page
- within .05 microns
- in 18–20 minutes
- so that it is level
- at A equals 440 pitch
- with exact correspondence

2. *Ask the trainee a direct question, such as:*

- What is the difference between? . . .
- When would you need this?
- Who else needs to know?
- Where does this belong?
- Why is this important?

Tie your questions to the several behavioral objectives you've listed on the lesson plan so that both you and the trainee know that together you've accomplished that task. In one-to-one training, a raised eyebrow, intense eye contact, or an inquiring smile can often bring the response you're looking for from your trainee.

3. *Give the trainee a specified amount of private time to practice or to figure things out*. For example, tell him that in seven minutes you'll be back to see how he is doing. Stick to your time limit; come back and check your trainee's work,

talking out loud as you do so that the trainee can see the critical decision points that you go through.

4. *Don't let the trainee go forward until your criteria have been met.* If the instruction has failed, be prepared to present it again in another way, or be prepared to take another look at the behavioral objective and perhaps break it down into several even smaller objectives. Learning is a two-way responsibility—the instructor's and the trainee's. Good instruction is always designed; it doesn't just happen. Stay focused on your objectives for the trainee. Measure success often during instruction in many small ways. Together with your trainee, check off completed items in your task checklist.

Student Evaluations

Even in one-to-one training, it's a good idea to have a formal student evaluation or feedback form for the trainee to fill out at the end of training. This evaluation will give you information that will make your next attempt at instruction even better. There are two ways to do this, the simplest being a feedback meeting directly after the instruction is finished. The other way is to use a written form, similar to the kind used after group training.

If you use a written form, keep it to one page, and seek information for training improvement. Don't just go for a "smiles test" or seek a pat on the back. Ask specific questions that get to the heart of how you designed this training experience. Always give your trainee space on the form or on the back of it to write some comments. Always ask the trainee to elaborate, especially in problem areas.

These are some of the items you might include on a written student evaluation form:

_____   Were the objectives realistic? [*Ask for specific information on any that you were not sure about.*]

_____ Was everything covered that needed to be covered? [*List topics that you're particularly curious about, and ask the trainee to elaborate.*]

_____ Was the training situation conducive to learning? [*Ask for specific suggestions for improvement.*]

_____ Did the instructor present information clearly? [*Ask for constructive comments.*]

Written responses are preferable to simply discussing the course. This is because you want the trainee to know when training has stopped and when you return to your normal manager-employee relationship. Formalizing the trainee feedback by using a written evaluation form helps establish this point of change.

How to Receive Feedback From Your Trainee (Subordinate)

There are a few basic rules about receiving feedback:

1. *Be sure your trainee knows that you want him to be honest.* This is an exercise in improving training. Keep it in the realm of training, and this specific training, so that the trainee doesn't get flustered at the thought of possibly telling the boss he messed up.
2. *Accept feedback for what it is—feedback.* Don't explain or try to defend your position if the feedback isn't quite what you wanted to hear.
3. *Probe to clarify.* Especially if you are in a face-to-face meeting, ask probing questions about only the point of the immediate discussion (for example, content—"What additional information would you like?" "Which steps would be most useful to the next person?" "How would you rearrange those items?"
4. *Don't let the giver of feedback get carried away.* It's your job to keep the feedback session on target. Don't allow personal digressions into personality problems or general gripes. Stick to the business of training evaluation.

Scheduling Tricks

Although it's hard to schedule one-to-one training—because when you have a situation that requires it, you probably have a one-of-a-kind trainee whom you would rather have at work than in class—there are some scheduling tricks you can use to minimize the time that person spends away from the job.

1. *Come early . . . stay late.* Most people who realize that they need training are willing to use some of their own time as long as the company is willing to use some of its time to get the job done. If your trainee is a morning person who is wide awake when she comes to work and who likes to do a lot of work in the mornings, you generally will have no argument if you ask that person to come half an hour early one or two days in order to get the training. If you design a one-hour session for one or two days, that means you meet the person half-way and give up some of your time too. If the training takes longer than you planned and you have to request more early days, consider granting the trainee some compensatory time later at her convenience. Often, when you need a trained employee in a hurry, the compensatory time option is a good option that allows you to schedule the training time right away to fit your work requirements and productivity goals.

A variation of the "come early" schedule is the "stay late" schedule. This works best with a night person or one who tends to wake up slowly in the morning. Most trainees will not object to having to stay for an extra half hour or hour in order to get the training that's required. Again, if the training requires more than two or three late sessions, consider granting compensatory time at the employee's convenience.

2. *See you at lunch!* If car pools or train schedules prevent your trainee from coming early or staying late, suggest a lunchtime training session. Have lunch sent in from a neighborhood sandwich shop, local supermarket soup and salad bar, or the company cafeteria.

Extend the training session by 20 minutes to allow enough time to socialize a bit while eating, and eat your lunch at the same time with the trainee during training. Remember, you're in this together! Give your training a catchy title like "Salad Bar Seminar." Be sure the trainee knows that it's training and not just lunch with the boss.

If lunchtime training becomes a regular thing, you can suggest that trainees bring their own lunch on those days. Bring your own lunch too. Send out your training reminder under the notice "Bag More Than Lunch." Be sure that everyone concerned knows that training will be happening during this particular lunch hour. Send the message that interruptions and socializing are not welcome during this time.

3. *Every day. . . .* When your training will take five to ten hours, try to schedule it for five consecutive days, for example, Monday through Friday from 11:00 A.M. until 12:30 P.M. or from 3:00 P.M. to 5:00 P.M. daily. Choose a time during the work day when productivity typically falls off or when you can afford to be away from your regular job of managing the operation. You'll probably gain more in regular productive work from your trainee (and from yourself) by sticking to a regular training schedule. Try to avoid calling the person away from work just because you have a few minutes to spare. This denigrates the importance of training.

4. *Once a week. . . .* Your training might be the kind that requires the trainee to go back to the job and practice new skills or integrate new knowledge and wait for feedback from his peers before you can go on to the next step in training. Your objectives might be stated in such a way that trial and error are required before you can assess whether or not your trainee has succeeded in learning.

If this is the case, schedule training at regular intervals, for example once a week for the next four weeks or until you judge that training has been accomplished. Again, let the trainee know that training is being conducted during this time period, and that his learning will be assessed at the end of the period. Always convey the message that training is something special and different from the work itself. Training has a beginning and an end, a specific purpose, and specific measurements associated with it. Be sure your trainee knows when you step in and out of your role as instructor. A firm schedule will help define training and clarify the roles.

5. *Feathering*. On occasion, you may have several one-to-one trainees going at once. This could happen when you have two clerical employees starting the same day on different equipment—a word processing specialist and a computer graphics specialist, for example, or three retail clerks in the same department but responsible for different product lines.

In such situations, in order to maximize the time they can spend covering their assignments, to optimize the time each gives to training, and to keep your instructional functions straight, you might want to consider feathering their training time. This means developing one-to-one lesson plans for each individual since each person's needs, content, and objectives will be basically different, but overlapping their training times with you in common areas. Feather one person's time into another's time for learning skills or information common to all trainees.

This can be done by using a videotape of yourself set up in one of their offices or in an empty room, so that all trainees can view it at designated times and then have private time one-to-one with you. While one person is viewing the tape, the next person is with you. Scheduling is then reversed, and you've accomplished perhaps three hours of training in only an hour and a half of your time. This can also be done by scheduling a viewing session for all the trainees together. Or you can take the time to deliver a five-minute minilecture, demonstration, or flipchart explanation in your office to all of them at once as long as they all need to know that same content.

Time Savers

The reality of being a manager often is that the varied pressures of work and people problems mean that you need to take shortcuts in key functions such as training. The following sections show some ways to save time and still design and deliver effective training.

Structured Self-Study

One way to save instructional time is to develop a task list self-assessment sheet for the trainee, with a specified mastery level or success criterion for each task, such as the one shown in Figure 3. Have the trainee begin working through the list, documenting on the recording sheet as tasks are completed at a mastery or criterion level. Structure the trainee's self-study.

Build into the self-study some regular check-in times with you so that you can be sure the trainee is meeting or at least working toward meeting the objectives you've set. A task list can be combined with a self-assessment recording sheet and put onto a clipboard so that the trainee gets the feeling that what's on that clipboard is special and requires a different kind of focus than that given regular work assignments.

Briefing, Debriefing, and Life Experience

You may be faced with such a time crunch that you really can't afford the time to do training, but you know that an individual needs some attention in order to do the assigned work better. One approach to solving this dilemma is the concept of using key questions to focus an employee's thinking and actions during a specified period of time.

For example, you might have an employee whose job is to review state reports, pick out the important points, and write up an executive summary for you. Lately, you feel that this employee has been missing important information and the quality of your executive summaries has slipped in consequence. You don't have time to train her, but you can come up with some analysis guidelines that you believe will get the job back on track if she follows them over the next few weeks. You present the employee with four key questions to consider as she analyzes each new state report. For example: How does the committee's action reflect policy #4231? Who are the lobbyists? Which counties have pending legal action? What is the nature of each county's legal action? In this case, it has taken you only ten minutes to write down the key questions and have a brief

Figure 3. Task list/self-assessment sheet.

Job: _____			
Tasks	Performance Level Desired	Performance Level Attained	Date
1 _____	_____	_____	_____
2 _____	_____	_____	_____
3 _____	_____	_____	_____
4 _____	_____	_____	_____
5 _____	_____	_____	_____
6 _____	_____	_____	_____
7 _____	_____	_____	_____
8 _____	_____	_____	_____

conversation with your employee in which you suggest using them for the next three weeks. In this kind of time-saving one-to-one encounter, you are the training designer, but the employee really trains herself.

You can use this time-saving technique in a briefing meeting in which you and the employee get together just long enough for you to present the questions and start the person off in the right direction. Agree to reconvene at a certain time—in a few hours, a few days, or a few weeks—and to use the same questions as a frame of reference for how the work went, that is, in a debriefing session. Give the employee feedback during the debriefing about her choices of action and accomplishments, tying together the briefing session and the debriefing session by means of the key questions. This kind of session also need take only a few minutes.

Another related time saver is a meeting with your trainee to focus on his life experiences on or off the job, at this company or at another, as they may relate to the new job challenge. By guiding him in thinking about his past, you can often inspire your employee to apply to the new task the same skills or ways of approaching a challenge that he successfully used in past performance. Adults are amazingly resourceful because of their tremendous memory store of information. Sometimes all they need is a memory-jogger, like a focused conversation with their boss-turned-trainer, to propel them into a repeat or enhancement of a previous success.

Job Aids

A job aid is a card, folder, model, template, wall chart, or other tangible device to assist a worker in performing his job. Job aids are often simplified versions of a user guide or job manual. They usually contain instructions or step-by-step procedures, and often illustrate a work process through a flowchart or by a graphic representation of a physical system or process, such as an electrical system or a chemical process. A job aid could be a model, with the important parts labeled or highlighted. A decision chart, featuring a column of "ifs" and a corresponding column of "thens," often becomes a job aid posted on the wall. A sales tax chart at a retail store becomes a job aid for employees who ring up customers' purchases at a cash register.

One-to-one training can be greatly facilitated by job aids. But if you rely on a job aid with your trainee, check it carefully to be sure it is accurate, current, and exactly corresponds to the methods or systems you require of that trainee on the job. The problem with job aids is that unless you yourself design them, they run the risk of being just a little off the mark in terms of your own specific training approach or training needs. They can be great time savers; just be sure you take a few minutes to check them out before you use them.

Selected Sample Situations

This section reviews five familiar one-to-one training situations, and gives you suggestions for dealing with them. Each situation is presented as a situation requiring a one-to-one training solution; though the reason why this solution is required is specific to each case, the training design for all such situations can be approached from a similar perspective.

The key components of a sample lesson plan are suggested for each different training situation. In your own training, use these examples to guide you in creating as many 15-minute lesson plans as you need.

1: Your New Assistant

Staff turnover is a common reason for finding yourself with a new employee. In this case, your assistant is leaving and has agreed to help train his replacement. You need his help in training the new employee, but you want to be sure your new assistant learns what you want taught, not just what your previous assistant wants to teach her. This clearly is a situation where you should control the training design. Never make the mistake of allowing a subordinate to develop and control work procedures and systems that he alone understands. Unless you are on top of the systems, your assistant may well become the indispensable person in the department—a situation that will be encouraged by your failure to intervene.

At turnover time, be especially aware of your opportunities as a manager to reevaluate the essential tasks of the job that's being turned over. Sit down with your current assistant and construct a task list. By all means, get his input based on the experience he's had doing the job. Find out what's hard and what's not so hard to accomplish. Study that list, add other tasks to it, or modify those already on the list. Use this point of change as an opportunity to examine your goals for the position—even if things have been going extremely smoothly.

Overall Purpose of Training, Sample Situation 1

Over the next three weeks, to learn the procedure for processing the ten different financial products available to clients through the office of the Vice-President of Investments.

Lesson title: Placing Stock Orders

Purpose of this lesson: To demonstrate correct procedures for placing a stock order

Materials needed for this lesson: Client Interaction Checklist, three blank order forms, one sample client profile

Behavioral objectives for this lesson:

1. The trainee will be able to tell me when I ask her at any time during the last half of the lesson what the three absolutely essential first steps are.
2. During role play with me as the client, the trainee will be able to converse appropriately, as indicated by use of at least four out of the six items on the Client Interaction Checklist.
3. Using actual data, the trainee will be able to fill out all the paperwork required to place an order.

Content outline for this lesson:

1. Step-by-step procedures for placing stock orders:
   a. Overview of legal and technical requirements
   b. Three absolutely essential first steps
   c. Procedures used only occasionally

2. Client interaction checklist
3. Data sheets and order form

2: Your Successor

In this situation, you are leaving a managerial job and must train your successor. You probably will have only a very short time—several hours, not several weeks—in which to do the training.

You'll probably begin by thinking about what the new person needs to know; that is, you'll begin thinking about major chunks of content. Force yourself to think at the same time in terms of behaviors that are related to that content. Your successor undoubtedly has access to the same sources of content as you do, but what he lacks are the behaviors or "how tos" of the job that you have found to be critical skills. It's those critical management skills that you'll want to share with your successor during the time you have available for training. Make the most of the training time by not getting bogged down in content.

In this kind of training, you should discipline yourself to think in terms of a lesson plan, although you probably will not take lesson plans with you to lunch. It's far more likely that you'll make a few notes on an index card and put it in your pocket as a reminder. Use the lesson plan as a guide, jotting down behaviors and key items of content.

Overall Purpose of Training, Sample Situation 2

During three extended lunches next week, to develop an appreciation for the nuances of the problem of dedicated machine time.

Lesson title: (lunch #2) Conflicting Users

Purpose of this lesson: To define the problem

Materials needed for this lesson: None

Behavioral objectives for this lesson:

1. To identify all of the users, not just the obvious ones
2. To categorize use by business priority

3. To discuss prevailing usage standards

Content outline for this lesson:

1. Users
2. Machine Capacity
3. Job Design and Work Flow
4. Standards

3: Same Person, New Job

You often find yourself in the situation of having just given one of your employees added job responsibilities or a different job within your organization. One example might be the secretary who is now a customer service rep. You need to train her to do the specific tasks of the new job. This may involve some attitude training as well as training in the skills and new information that she must have to be a good customer service rep.

Overall Purpose of Training, Sample Situation 3

To demonstrate the ability to perform customer service functions expected of level 1 reps. Six 30-minute training sessions are planned during the next ten days, covering shipment confirmation, complaint processing, complaint resolution, product advice, and special orders.

Lesson title: Product Advice

Purpose of this lesson: To demonstrate at least four appropriate responses to customers when they ask for product advice.

Materials needed for this lesson: Product Advice Wall Chart; audio cassette (30-minute) and cassette player to record the trainee's responses to the role play (when I'm the "customer"); logon and password to the on-line product information system

Behavioral objectives for this lesson:

1. To access the on-line product information system
2. To identify the seven features of product inquiry

3. To demonstrate appropriate responses to customer inquiries during a role play featuring looking up actual product information in the current system

Content outline for this lesson:

1. Accessing the on-line product information system
2. Seven features of product inquiry (person's name, telephone number, address, product stock numbers, color, size, availability)
3. Taped role play and responses
4. Replay of the tape for the trainee

4: A Personal Computer

You may have to train someone to use a personal computer—in the event that higher management decides that every department needs PCs, or every assistant manager is going to be issued a PC, or every line of business is now required to use the same spreadsheet or project management software. It looks like the worst-case scenario: PC training is not your favorite thing to do, your trainee is bound to be nervous, and your boss's boss is watching like a hawk to see how the PCs are being integrated throughout the company. This scene is so common in businesses today that it's worth a few extra pages to set your mind at ease and to give you some tips about how to do this kind of training one-to-one.

Even if you don't know all there is to know about the PC, there are some simple things you as a manager can do to get the training going. Often, with PC training, that's all you have to do—get it going. PC users generally become very attached to their PCs early in the relationship, and they tend to train themselves with time to experiment. Often your attitude is as important as the technical training itself in the new PC user's training.

Don't expect miracles. Think of worst-case scenarios first. If your trainee doesn't know how to type, that's a big problem. If your trainee can't sit still and focus, that's a problem. If your trainee has eyeglasses that are geared for work at a desk flat out in front and not to a screen sticking up in space, that's a problem. If your trainee can't stand the ever-present hum of a fan inside the computer or just doesn't relate well to machines, that's a problem. All these kinds of problems have to be solved before you can get down to training someone to use a PC.

Your job as manager-turned-trainer in one-to-one PC training is similar to your job as a trainer in any other kind of training: find out what the learner needs to know in the way of knowledge, attitudes, and skills. Remember that one-to-one training especially requires that you start from where the learner is, in terms of experience, information, and beliefs about the learning situation.

In PC training, you might have to function as a training coordinator for an individual, sending that worst-case trainee to a typing course first, or keeping the machine in the packing crate until your trainee gets a new pair of eyeglasses. You might have to pair up your reluctant trainee with a seasoned PC user for a few days so that she can watch the old pro at work with the objective of modifying your trainee's negative attitude toward or fear of the PC. Meet your individual trainee at her individual level of concern before you begin talking about files, commands, and functions.

Learn about the content of your trainee's job too before you begin training in the operation of the new PC. Find out how the person actually does her job now. Help your trainee develop a mental framework of steps, procedures, guiding principles, concepts, and shortcuts to doing the job. Go slowly through this exercise, reinforcing the trainee's logic and good decision making. Point out elements of the current job that can be made faster, easier, more complete, or more elegant by using the PC.

Be sure your trainee knows her current job well before attempting to "computerize" that job and that person. Remember that the computer will do only what it's told to do. Be sure that your trainee thoroughly understands the standard information organizers that the new software uses—for example, charts, matrices, outlines, tree structures, formulas, steps, addresses. Clear up any misunderstandings and supply any missing information in conversation or on paper first. Give your trainee her best shot at accepting the computer as a tool.

Do your own homework first. Try out the software on a typical problem that your trainee might use the PC to solve, or use a set of data that your trainee will recognize. Be sure that the software is at the right level for this person. For example, if there's a tutorial built into it, be sure that it's neither insulting to your employee's intelligence by being too elementary, nor too difficult. Be sure that the software is user-friendly for your particular user.

Also find out where to get help. Find out who the PC gurus in your company are, who runs the best software-specific courses and when they will be given, how much in the way of handholding and user support you can get from the manufacturer or distributor of the PC you purchased, and who else in the company is using the same software for an application similar to your trainee's. Have this information written down, ready to pass on to your trainee. Do as much as you possibly can to remove the fear of failure and the loneliness that often surround the new PC user.

When you are satisfied that your trainee is ready to get acquainted with the new PC, set aside a private space and plenty of time for the introduction. Assemble all the printed materials neatly and in a place where the trainee can easily reach them. Encourage hands-on use early in the training, but don't remove the printed "crutches." Help the trainee relate new verbal instructions to specific pages in the reference documents or user manual so that she feels some sense of confidence about solving her own problems later without having to call you back.

If at all possible, have the PC plugged in and hooked up to a printer, the operating system already loaded, backup disks already formatted, and the software ready to be used. That is, make your first session an applications session if possible. New PC users don't have enough experience to know how to differentiate computer terminology or how to match up what information goes with which part of learning. It's very easy for new PC users to confuse operating system information with software operation, to confuse functions with commands. New users don't have to know all the features and wonderful possibilities of their new PC; they should not open the user's guide to page one and start reading; they just need to know how to make the machine work for them.

If you can, begin your first session of one-to-one PC training by loading the applications software. Talk your trainee through which keys to press and why. Help your trainee work backwards into problem solution if she gets into trouble. Laugh with her at stupid mistakes; tell her why they are stupid mistakes. Work with your trainee to exercise the machine; look up the various options the menu presents. Give the trainee plenty of time, with you constantly guiding and prodding, to explore the PC's capabilities within a familiar application. Return to hardware and system issues at later training sessions. Give your trainee time to experiment on her own. Be on call, not as a manager, but as a follow-up instructor, during the initial weeks of new PC use after the training is finished.

As in other kinds of one-to-one training, have a plan, have a specified training time, and be totally devoted to training during the time you are with your trainee. As in other kinds of training, plan 15-minute lessons, and check your learner several times during that lesson to verify mastery of the new knowledge or skill.

Overall Purpose of Training, Sample Situation 4

In the next hour, to learn to move, copy, delete, and restore text within a file. To practice on newly created documents and on previously created documents.

Lesson title: Rearranging Text Within a File

Purpose of this lesson: To navigate within a file to rearrange text

Materials needed for this lesson: Text processing software disc, last Monday's copy of the corporate "Network News Briefs" (to practice on)

Behavioral objectives for this lesson:

1. To use menu options for rearranging text
2. To move text
3. To copy text
4. To delete and restore deleted text

Content outline for this lesson:

1. The main menu and help screens
2. Moving text
3. Copying text
4. Deleting and restoring text

5: English as a Second Language

Societal changes reflected in changes in your pool of workers may require you to train someone for whom English is a second language. Sometimes these changes are mandated by policy statements regarding equal employment opportunity and affirmative action. Training someone who is not proficient in English can be a special challenge to a manager. Helping this kind of trainee to learn often has spinoff rewards in the human relations area such as better communication, better understanding of cultural diversity, and increased respect for that person's ability to rise above obstacles.

This kind of training involves a heavy dose of knowledge training and tends to be ongoing. Like the other sample situations, it too requires a special time to be set aside for training. When trying to integrate a person with language deficiencies into your department, it's tempting to want to be teaching that person constantly. Be careful of this temptation, because if you treat the newcomer as one who always needs training, you are probably not being fair. After all, you have hired a person with skills and abilities. Let those shine through. Step into your trainer role intentionally and with a plan for language lessons.

Approach this kind of training on a very individual basis, asking the trainee exactly where he needs help with English in order to function more productively on the job. Like any other learner, this person will have strengths and weaknesses. Speaking without an accent might be a major goal, or writing subjects and verbs that agree might be the objective. Spelling might be the major problem, or it might be the proper use of prepositions. Each person's needs will be different.

When you have figured out what kinds of training are needed, then decide if you have the skills to do the training. Chances are that you can do most of it, but you may have to call in an English teacher or teacher who specializes in teaching English to persons for whom English is a second language (ESL).

Whether you do the training or bring in help, keep the subject matter of your lessons job-related. If you teach a lesson on writing sentences in which subjects and verbs agree, use a department report or memo as an example. Copy the style of an acceptable company publication as you analyze and reproduce writing. If you are teaching the fine points of doing a presentation, choose a subject that is very familiar to the trainee. Create as little cognitive dissonance as you can during the time a trainee is trying to translate language and recast rules of communication and expression. Keep your training sessions to no longer than one hour at a time.

There are several tricks you can use to teach knowledge, or concepts:

1. State several key characteristics of the concept (for example, the concepts of clauses, prepositional phrases, a memo, a proposal).
2. Give examples of the concept in the context of the trainee's job.
3. Suggest examples of what the concept is not (choosing examples from the person's job); compare and contrast what it is and what it isn't.

Use audiotape and videotape to let the trainee hear and see you, other speakers, and himself. Expand the trainee's exposure to language in a laboratory setting. Supervise the trainee's practice. Encourage the trainee to record himself on audiotape at home or in the car on the way to work. Be sure each training session is private until the trainee gives you an indication that he is ready to try out the new language learning on others. Encourage the trainee to listen to news broadcasters on radio and TV and to analyze their speech patterns, pronunciation, and development of ideas. Talk about the trainee's observations during your lessons. Make your language lessons as job-related and as "adult" as you can. Be very careful that remedial training does not make your trainee feel second-class.

Overall Purpose of Training, Sample Situation 5

Every Friday during the next two months, to work on writing memos in an acceptable style based on that used in the company technical style manual. At the end of the two-month period, to write a "real" memo and send it to the appropriate person in the company.

Lesson title: Asking for Information

Purpose of this lesson: To analyze four common ways of requesting information in a memo

Materials needed for this lesson: Style manual

Behavioral objectives for this lesson:

1. To find the appropriate section in the style manual
2. To compare and contrast the four common ways of requesting information in a memo
3. To choose two of these that I am willing to try
   a. List the good points about these two choices.
   b. Tell why I think I can do these two and why I might have trouble with the other two ways.

Content outline for this lesson:

1. Style manual, sections 7a, 7b, 7c, 7d
2. Business conventions regarding requesting information (spoken, informal, across levels, peer to peer)
3. Differences between a memo and other written communications requesting information

In Brief

The five sample one-to-one training situations give you specific examples of when you might choose this kind of delivery of training and what might go into its design. One-to-one training can be the most efficient and effective way to deliver training, leading to enhanced personal performance and increased individual productivity.

The following checklist can help you train employees one-to-one.

MANAGER'S CHECKLIST 2

How to Train Employees One-to-One

_____ 1. Step into your role as a trainer by extending your role as a leader. Guide, show, and facilitate.

_____ 2. Focus on the learning objectives of this specific trainee. Think in terms of knowledge, attitudes, and skills required.

_____ 3. Ask the trainee what he needs to know.

_____ 4. Choose a good time for training and consistently stick to your established schedule. Be sure training is different from just a friendly conversation at work.

_____ 5. Present the big picture first; review the requirements of the job; build on what the trainee already knows and can do.

_____ 6. Give clues; give practice time; encourage trial and error; give feedback; plan for follow-up after training.

_____ 7. Make the training space comfortable.

_____ 8. Take care in preparing handout materials. Go for quality, even with only one student.

_____ 9. Be alert for situations where you have to function as a training broker or coordinator, yet still carry the major instructional responsibility.

_____ 10. Plan 15-minute lessons. Write lesson plans. Think small. Focus on helping your trainee to accomplish small steps of new behavior tied to specific small elements of content.

_____ 11. Ask your trainee for written feedback about the training and your presentation of it.

_____ 12. Don't confuse supervision with instruction. Be very clear about when you are performing the function of instructor and about when that function stops.

CHAPTER 3

How to Use Peer Training

Often a manager can delegate one-to-one training to someone else. This chapter examines the advantages and possibilities of training an individual by using that person's colleague or peer as the trainer.

Of course, as the manager of both these people, you still have ultimate responsibility for how that training is conducted and for the degree to which the trainee becomes fully productive after the training is over. In this kind of training, too, you have to be a facilitator, although your role is that of an administrative or managerial facilitator, not that of a facilitator of learning per se, as you are when you yourself function as the trainer.

In peer training, you delegate the important instructional role to a subordinate. By doing this, you gain many benefits, but you assume some different responsibilities regarding identifying and training that peer. You also share some of your own managerial leadership functions as you entrust that trainee's learning to your subordinate.

This chapter shows you how to make good decisions regarding

peer training, and helps you to see the management benefits of it. You'll learn how to choose the right kind of person to be a peer trainer, how to make the most of subject matter experts, how competence figures in, and what's involved in apprentice training. You'll also get some practical guidelines on training your peer trainer to develop and teach lessons. Five sample situations illustrate various techniques in peer training.

What's the Payoff?

The learning benefits of peer training are similar to the benefits of one-to-one training when you are the trainer. These benefits include highly effective learning, efficient learning, and savings in money and time. In addition to these, there are some special benefits of peer training: sharing your management responsibility, transmitting work values from peer to peer, and providing the potential for motivating, inspiring through role modeling, and instilling a healthy sense of competition within the trainee.

Shared Management Responsibilities

As most managers realize, those who delegate or share some of their management responsibilities generally more than make up for any loss of control by the positive attitudes and increased motivation engendered in the employees entrusted with additional responsibility. Training is one of the management functions that can often be delegated to a high-performing subordinate.

When you do this, limit the subordinate's number of trainees to one or two so that the instructional design principles discussed in one-to-one training can also be applied to creating lessons in peer training. Being an instructor is hard work largely because of the intensely personal nature of the interaction between teacher and learner and because of the pressure to perform work better.

Another kind of management payoff to using peer training is the ongoing benefit of demonstrating to your employees that you are a person who believes in the power of people, of shared experiences, and of mediation in important work processes rather than in do-or-die directives. An organization that sees that you believe in it by valuing the know-how of your subordinates will probably be socialized in a different, more collegial way from an organization that sees only top-down management control. An organization that sees that you as a manager can take the time to encourage sharing of ideas instead of dictating solutions can be expected to continue sharing ideas, allowing time for puzzles to remain puzzles, thoughts and solutions to incubate for awhile, and inspiration to develop. Peer training, even during those times when you could just as easily do it yourself, is often the preferred training method for these organizational development reasons.

Transmission of Values

Obviously you want to choose a peer trainer carefully. The peer trainer should be a high performer, one whom you trust to represent the company well during instructional sessions, and one whose values regarding work and his own particular job are the same as yours.

The transmission of work values is even more likely to take place under peer training than when you yourself are the instructor. This is because of the general tendency of people at work to seek comrades, and "we're in this together" thinking is encouraged by the peer training relationship. When that peer trainer solidly represents the values you represent, the transmission of values to the trainee is doubly strong. Peer training is a very powerful vehicle for instilling corporate and work values and for ensuring their continuation.

Motivation, Aspiration, and Competition

Another important payoff of peer training is more highly motivated employees. This generally happens because trainer and trainee constantly interact, giving each other feedback about how each is doing. Generally, this feedback engenders feelings of satisfaction and accomplishment that come from working toward common goals. What you typically find in peer training is a peer trainer who gets good strokes from the trainee and a peer trainee who gets good strokes from the trainer. People who feel good about what they're doing and how they're progressing usually keep going in the positive direction. Often in peer training, the trainer experiences the same feelings of success the trainee does. There is mutual concern and often increased self-esteem in both the trainer and the trainee.

Another effect can be expected from peer training. Very often during the course of training the trainee will develop an aspiration to be like the peer trainer. The peer trainer becomes not only a teacher but a worker role model as well. A trainee who sees by a criterion-referenced task list that the peer instructor can do certain job tasks to a high level of proficiency tends to get the message that this is how the job is supposed to be done. If the training goes well, chances are that the trainee will aspire to do the job the same way. Chances are that the trainee will view the trainer as a friend to consult in times of confusion or trouble later. Chances are that through peer training, you can build a sharing and cooperating organization that motivates itself to go forward.

Peer training can also bring about a healthy sense of competition between the participants. After the initial peer training is completed, the trainee may decide that he can exceed the criterion levels attained during training; or perhaps develop suggestions on how to do the job better or on how to enrich the previous guidelines. Don't be surprised if peer training leads to higher standards.

Who's the Right Peer?

One way to find out who among your high performers might like to be a peer tutor is to ask them. You'd be surprised at who gives you a positive response. Don't make any assumptions about who is the best candidate; it's not always the brainiest, or even the most outgoing, who should be chosen for the task. The shy person may open up when called on to teach, and patience becomes an obvious virtue in the context of instructing others. Sometimes individuals have certain biases that prevent them from being effective instructors. You'll need to find out if this is the case before you embark upon a peer training program.

Self-Assessment

The following guidelines can be used in several ways. You can post them on an employee bulletin board as a constant reminder to anyone who might want to be a peer trainer. You can enclose them in a memo you send around to a handful of people whom you consider potential peer trainers. You can make them into a self-test, giving the potential peer trainer a chance to ''agree'' or ''disagree'' with each guideline presented. (All items should be checked ''agree'' if the person is to be comfortable and successful as a peer trainer.) But no matter which way you choose to present the guidelines for employee self-assessment, be sure that you interview the potential peer trainers around these guidelines before you make your choice.

PEER TRAINER SELF-ASSESSMENT

	Agree	*Disagree*
1. I believe that every individual at work is capable of learning.	☐	☐
2. Individuals learn at different rates.	☐	☐
3. Getting involved in learning by trial and error and hands-on experience is the way in which most adults want to learn.	☐	☐
4. Working toward standards, criteria, or specifications helps both the trainer and the trainee to measure progress.	☐	☐

5. Giving positive reinforcement many times during a lesson is a good idea. ☐ ☐
6. Adult learners appreciate the opportunity to tell you how they learn best and what they need to know. ☐ ☐
7. I like to share with others what I know. ☐ ☐

Personality Guidelines

You'll want a peer trainer to be proud of being a teacher. There's a good bit of courage that is demonstrated during peer training lessons—courage on the part of the learner to risk looking foolish, and courage on the part of the teacher to let valuable time be expended in order to present a concept in several different ways or to allow the trainee to practice until the lesson is understood. Your peer trainer has to be willing to deal with these issues of exposure and delay in order to accomplish learning goals.

Your peer trainer should be a person who takes pride in his work, not one who works just to get paid. Both kinds of workers could very well be high performers, but you want to build into your peer training that extra sense of appreciation of standards, not just awareness of standards.

Finally, your peer trainer should be someone who can stand the attention of a fellow worker. Some people like to be left alone at work so they can just get on with their jobs. The peer trainer, by contrast, takes on the added identification of coach, troubleshooter, and helper. The peer trainer has to be someone who can tolerate the possible jealousy of fellow workers because of the extra dimensions of the job that now set him a little apart. Some perfectly good candidates for peer trainer simply don't like the spotlight. You'll want to choose someone who likes to share ideas and techniques for improving work.

The peer trainer has to be self-confident but not egotistical. Someone with quiet self-confidence is what you're looking for, not a noisy extroverted braggart. It's tempting when choosing a person to perform as a teacher to think first of a "showman" who can manipulate a crowd with clever talk and really get a point across. That's not what a teacher is, and it certainly is not what the intensely personal peer training situation requires. Your peer trainer has to be self-assured and demonstrate confidence that comes from competence. The peer trainer has to be able to look a fellow worker in the eye and say, "No, that's not right, and here's why. . . ." But he does not have to be an entertainer or a show-off.

Work Record

Your peer trainer should have an outstanding work record, in terms of attendance, attitudes, and performance. Above all, you want your peer trainer to know his or her job "backwards and forwards." You'll want someone who absolutely and thoroughly understands the standards for good performance of this particular job.

You'll want someone who has internalized the daily disciplines of the job—for example, someone who has the routines down pat, someone who is organized about the things that matter to the job, someone who quickly focuses on the tasks of the job in the right sequence, someone who knows just where to go for helpful information, someone who doesn't get distracted. You'll want someone who usually does it right the first time.

Your peer trainer doesn't necessarily have to be an old-timer on the job. Someone relatively new can often be an excellent peer trainer. As a manager, don't make any assumptions about who's the best peer trainer; check people out first.

Special Peers: Subject-Matter Experts

Subject-matter experts know the content of their jobs very well and can tell you whatever you need to know about the domain, or subject, of their work. They are the ones to whom you'd go to be sure you included everything of importance in your content outline of training lessons; they are the ones who often get involved in setting standards; they are good human resources for test designers and for evaluators. A subject-matter expert is a worker with a very high potential for contribution if the organization values his subject as the "real work" of the organization.

Subject-matter experts may or may not be high performers in an organization, depending on how well they can turn their knowledge of content into useful work. Often a manager's greatest challenge is to figure out how to optimize the efforts of the subject-matter expert—how to communicate corporate values to him, how to protect the expert from becoming entangled in company politics, and how to create opportunities for contribution that might go beyond the contributions of employees with simply an average or more-than-acceptable command of content.

Subject-matter experts are usually defined by others; often they are appointed to become experts because of their potential to grow into a job; sometimes they become experts because they just happen to be in the right place at the right time to be noticed. They can be found at every level in an organization. A subject-matter expert may or may not be a good choice as a peer trainer.

Competence

Competent performance is the kind of performance a company values because its worth to the company is greater than the costs of achieving that performance. The competent worker will be a subject-matter expert who also instinctively understands the ways to go about dealing with the content, the effects of certain actions on that content, the approaches to analysis of that content, how to prioritize and connect parts of the content, and the procedures to use most effectively with that content to improve work. The competent worker knows how to accomplish many things within the framework of her content expertise.

The competent worker doesn't have to be taught the intuitive aspects of the job. She knows from experience how to recall the essential problem-solving information required on the job and can quickly and effectively sort through all the possible solutions to implement a fix. Through on-the-job experience, she stores and retrieves performance information in a way that's different from the worker who is not yet competent but can do many parts of the job. The competent worker recognizes useful patterns in situations related to the job, and takes less time and fewer resources to perform well. Competent workers make good on-the-job peer trainers.

Apprenticeship

Apprenticeship is a special kind of peer training that is governed by guidelines from the Department of Labor. If you want to start an apprenticeship program, contact the Bureau of Apprenticeship and Training of your State Labor Department. Your State Education Department might also be a good source of information and assistance regarding setting up the educational program and can provide persons who will talk with you about options for delivery of apprentice-related instruction.

Apprenticeship training is an on-the-job training opportunity leading to a career in a specific skilled trade. Only jobs appearing on the Department of Labor's list of apprenticeable occupations can figure in apprenticeship programs. Apprenticeship training has a very close relationship to the labor unions whose membership is composed of workers capable of meeting certain criteria. It is governed by federal laws such as the Fair Labor Standards Act, the Code of Federal Regulations regarding recruitment, selection, employment, and training of apprentices, equal employment opportunity and affirmative action legislation, federal and state wage laws, and local collective bargaining agreements, and is expected to follow any state guidelines regarding educational requirements. It leads to certification and credentialing and often union membership in a particular trade. Historically, apprenticeship has required 2,000 hours of supervised on-the-job training in the relevant occupation.

Apprentices are paid while they train under supervision on the job, and they are expected to have a certain number of hours (usually 144) of related theoretical education, often delivered in a classroom to a group of apprentices. Apprenticeship training is both a peer training program and a group training program. Apprenticeship training takes about three and a half years.

An effective apprenticeship program must be based on an organized, written plan stating the terms and conditions of employment, training, and supervision in an apprenticeable occupation. The plan must be endorsed by a sponsor, for example, your company, which agrees to develop and carry out the apprentice training. This requires a commitment from you of time, money, and paperwork coordination. The rewards can be many—a solidly skilled, competent worker, opportunities for you to learn about ways of planning training and about different ways of delivering instruction, a network of contacts in state government, and association with other skilled workers and apprentices in your geographic area.

Designs for Peer Training

Peer training design resembles one-to-one training design. It is the same as one-to-one training design when there is one peer instructor and one peer trainee, or one instructor and two trainees. Only when peer training involves one instructor and a group of trainees does the design differ, and then peer training follows the guidelines for group training (see Chapter 4).

Peer training most often is not group training. Group training is more difficult and requires more extensive training for the instructor in methods of teaching. Therefore, in this chapter, the emphasis is on peer training design to serve one or two peer trainees. The key train-the-trainer issues for peer training will be discussed in later sections of the chapter.

Lessons

As with one-to-one training, create lesson plans to use as the instructor guide for peer training. These lesson plans should be simple, brief, one-page guides to 15-minute sessions of training and learning. As in one-to-one training, keep the training time to about one hour of intense instruction. This means that the instructor will have four lesson plans for each training session.

Each 15-minute lesson plan should include:

- Title of the lesson
- Purpose of the lesson from the trainee's point of view
- Several behavioral objectives for the trainee
- A content outline of about four items
- A list of instructional aids or materials needed for this lesson

Peer training lesson plans should allow time for plenty of interaction between the peers. This will be reflected in the spareness and specificity of the objectives. In peer training, it sometimes takes a little more time to experiment and to explain. Don't be tempted to fill up the lesson plan with too many objectives or objectives that are unattainable. Think small in peer training; restrict the content list only to those items that are necessary for the trainee to accomplish the objectives of that 15-minute lesson. Don't be tempted to try to tell the trainee everything at once; work from small, specific objectives. If the training goes on for an extended time, as in apprentice training, put a series of lessons together into a cohesive unit of instruction. A group of units, then, becomes a course.

The following sections of this chapter will help you as a manager to help your peer trainer design lessons.

Knowledge, Attitudes, and Skills

Get your peer trainer to think about structuring training around the three basic kinds of learning: knowledge, attitudes, and skills (see Chapter 1). Be sure your peer trainer knows the difference between them. If you reviewed your peer trainer's lesson plans, would he be able to make it clear to you which objectives were knowledge objectives, which were attitude objectives, and which were skills objectives?

Having your peer trainer organize instruction around these three basic kinds of objectives makes it easier for you to follow up on training implementation later. If you, your trainer, and your trainee all know what the objectives are, you'll all be able to more reasonably and more effectively discuss the specific ways in which work is improving as a result of the training. You won't be tempted to evaluate a peer training skills objective by an attitudes standard, for example.

A list of typical objectives in each category might help your peer trainer in designing lessons:

Knowledge	Attitudes	Skills
Analyze	Accept	Assemble
Classify	Adopt	Bend
Compute	Agree	Focus
Define	Assert	Fold
Differentiate	Cooperate	Grasp
Interpret	Disagree	Lift
List	Prefer	Press
Modify	Support	Separate
Recall	Tolerate	Set
Specify	Value	Walk

Objectives and Task Lists

Help your peer trainer to get into the habit of thinking about his job as a working model of many correctly functioning parts. Get your trainer to think about the purpose or result of each task of the job, the structure or format of each task, and several ways of explaining or describing each task. Get the trainer to think about the specific tasks that need to be performed to some specific level of proficiency in order for work to be done well. Get your peer trainer to focus precisely on what it will take to teach someone else how to do each specific task.

Help your peer trainer to group the tasks appropriately under a specific objective. For example, the objective of confirming a reservation might involve the four tasks of speaking with the client on the telephone, cross-checking on a computer screen, entering new data into a reservation system, and filling out paperwork. Each of these separate tasks has to be taught and learned before the objective can be accomplished. Thinking about tasks as they relate to objectives will help the peer trainer to help the peer trainee to succeed in each task before going on to the next task. Listing and grouping all the tasks of a job are valuable aids to good instructional design.

The Monitoring Checklist

Your peer trainer should work from the task list to create a monitoring checklist for the time when a lesson is finished and the trainee demonstrates that she is able to do that task. Such a checklist should contain a listing of tasks down the left side of the page, a column of cues to watch for as the trainee demonstrates accomplishment, a rating scale, and a place for comments. You might want to suggest that the trainer hold the paper sideways to allow more space. How the monitoring checklist page should be set up is shown in Figure 4.

Group the tasks that fall into each objective to give your

Figure 4. Sample monitoring checklist page.

Task	Cues to Good Performance	Rating			Comments
		1	2	3	
1.					
2.					

1	Proficient at task.
2	Task needs practice.
3	Unsuccessful; must be repeated.

trainee a sense of direction during monitoring. Staple those pages together to make your job as evaluator easier. Remember, knowing that she is accumulating a series of small successes helps the trainee to continue learning. Share the completed monitoring checklist with your trainee.

A Word From the Peer Trainee

Remember that as manager you are responsible for both the peer trainer and the peer trainee. Be sure that you give the trainee a chance to evaluate the trainer. This can be done informally in a private discussion between you and the trainee, or through an evaluation form designed for this purpose. Whether you choose a discussion or a written form, give the trainee some structure within which to respond. After you synthesize the evaluation comments, share them with your peer trainer. Focus on training improvement as related to work improvement.

Ask the trainee about how the trainer performed the tasks of training. Suggest an attitude rating scale of from one to four, standing for "poor" to "excellent." Allow space on a written form for additional comments. A sample rating form appears in Figure 5.

The Schedule

A task list can be used to generate a peer training schedule. Once the job has been analyzed and its tasks isolated and defined, the tasks can be assigned to the time slots you have for training—this group of tasks for 3–4 P.M. Monday, this group of tasks for daily lessons during the week of August 10, and this group of tasks for the first month of training. If the peer trainer doesn't work from a task list, it will be very hard for him to have a realistic idea of how long the training will take. Your peer trainer might have some trouble developing the task list and using it to generate a schedule; be available to help if necessary.

Figure 5. Sample peer trainee evaluation form.

Describes and explains new ideas	1	2	3	4
Demonstrates procedures and skills	1	2	3	4
Provides useful and timely feedback	1	2	3	4
Answers questions	1	2	3	4
Is patient	1	2	3	4
Uses a variety of instructional methods	1	2	3	4
Overall rating of this peer trainer	1	2	3	4

Comments: _____

_____

_____

Training the Trainer

Your biggest responsibility in peer training is to train your peer trainer to be a teacher in addition to being a co-member with your peer trainee of a work group. The following sections of this chapter will help you to develop training skills in your peer trainer.

Guidelines for On-the-Job Peer Trainers

Peer training that takes place during the workday is more often known as on-the-job training. The generic principles discussed below apply to all training, but are geared particularly to the special conditions of the peer or colleague relationship. These guidelines are for your peer trainer to follow:

1. Describe the big picture of how your work (and the trainee's) contributes to the company's profitability. Establish yourselves as peers, working for the good of the company.

2. Indicate to the trainee that you value his presence in the organization.

3. Take the time to understand the trainee's enthusiasm for this particular work; try to put yourself in the same emotional frame of mind. Talk about where the trainee has come from, and where he wants to go with the job.

4. Be patient with the trainee's lack of understanding and with whatever fears he may have respecting the job or training. Look at these negatives as a wonderful opportunity for improvement.

5. Show—and tell. Demonstrate correct procedures, set up trial and error situations, show how things work; tell the trainee why certain ways of doing a task work or don't work.

6. Talk to the trainee when you exercise your intuition— when you review the trainee's work, when you go through a troubleshooting exercise, or when you analyze a risk. Get the trainee to see how you go about the task. Emphasize the critical points of decision.

7. Put the trainee in the position of being a trainer occasionally so that he can show you that a mastery of skills is taking place. Teaching is a very good way of forcing people to structure their thinking correctly. Give your trainee a chance to do this.

8. Allow the trainee to learn from mistakes. Take the time for the trainee to make some mistakes and then to figure out how to correct them. You'll know how far to go, and your trainee will learn what it takes never to do that again! When you review the trainee's incorrect performance, tell him what was wrong and why. Look at errors as opportunities for good teaching.

9. Encourage the trainee to ask questions.

10. Give specific feedback—what and why.

11. Separate elements of the job into small parts that can be described clearly and acted upon independently. Give the trainee a chance to accumulate small successes.

12. Keep your training schedule somewhat flexible so that you can adapt future lessons to the trainee's style and pace of learning. Be sure you can adjust your own work to do a good job of training.

13. Turn the trainee loose a little at a time. After he has demonstrated mastery of a specific task, let the trainee do this task on the job. Be available as a coach. Be sure the trainee and your boss know of the successful integration of training into actual job performance.

14. Have a clear end to training. Ask your boss to formalize it in some way—for example, by an end-of-training lunch, a certificate of completion, a wall plaque, or an article in the company newsletter. Reestablish your relationship as peer workers.

Balancing Formal and Informal Techniques

It will be tempting for your peer trainer to want to be friendly and informal as a teacher. Rather than thinking in terms of "friendly," try instead to get your peer trainer to think in terms of "open." Make it clear from the beginning that training is a special function of business, and must be governed by business guidelines such as relevance, efficiency, and effectiveness. "Friendly" is fine outside of training, but it often gets in the way of basic business goals.

Make it clear to your peer trainer that he must always be in control of the teaching and learning that's going on. This means that training has to follow a plan, and that the trainer has to engage in conscious teaching strategies. Planning and flexibility are the keys; the trainer must know where he is in the lesson and what's coming next, and must have a few alternative ways of presenting the lesson if the first try doesn't work.

Informality can detract from the clarity of a plan, and undermine the trainer's freedom to choose alternative presentation techniques. It's too tempting to go off on tangents when peer training is approached from too informal a perspective. It's easy to lose your place in a lesson plan and to waste time if you're joking around. Sharing and respect for a colleague are important concepts; interaction and feedback are essential; but informality is probably not the best environment in which to conduct peer training.

"Formal" does not mean stuffy, however. Formal simply means working from plans, having goals and objectives, evaluating work, and using evaluation results to improve the teaching and learning process in future sessions. Formal means having a structure, thoroughly understanding what that structure is, and operating within it. Teaching is a deliberate act. Learning never just happens. Quality, productivity, and competency don't just happen either. As a manager, set the right formal tone for peer training. Be sure to give your peer trainer enough time (days or weeks) to develop lessons, evaluation forms, task lists, and schedules. Check these plans and documents before peer training begins. Be flexible yourself in case training takes longer than you all imagined it would in the planning stage.

Using Media

Peer trainers may be tempted to think of their training task as "telling" the trainee everything. Try to get your peer trainer to think also of "helping" or "maneuvering" the trainee to learn most things for himself. Suggest to your peer trainer that the use of media can help him to become a facilitator. Media can be powerful aids to learning because they stimulate the subject's visual, auditory, and tactile senses simultaneously in a way that the written or spoken word cannot. Media can be very useful teaching tools for peer trainers because they expand the appeal of lessons. Media guidelines for group training are found in the next chapter.

Here are some guidelines for using media effectively in peer training:

1. Remember that media support instruction; they do not replace it. Don't be tempted to leave the trainee alone watching a video, for example. Stay with the trainee to watch his reactions

to key parts of the media presentation; be available to clarify or answer your trainee's questions.

2. Give your media a test run several days before training begins so that you have time to buy a spare bulb or extra extension cord or to discard outdated slides. Be sure your tapes are rewound and ready to use so you don't waste training time with your trainee. Be professional, even with only one or two trainees who happen to be your peers.

3. If you've never made use of flipcharts or overhead projectors or certain mockups or models in your teaching, practice the sections of your presentation in which they are key. Even if you have to practice in front of an empty chair, it's a good idea to do it just to give yourself a chance to talk and move around while managing the media at the same time. You don't want to end up blocking the trainee's view of the screen or blackboard or flipchart. Practice keeping eye contact with your "trainee" while you are moving around or demonstrating how a model works.

4. Encourage the trainee to interact with the media. Save some fill-in-the-blank type exercises for the trainee to do with you; have the trainee make a list on the flipchart of new procedures he has just learned; have the trainee work with you to get a model working or do a simulation with you. Use a good-quality 35mm camera to take closeup slides of processes or products ahead of time, and show them during training to give your trainee a sense of reality about your teaching. Enhance written or verbal instruction with media.

5. Use your imagination. Training should be appealing and fun.

6. Don't lose sight of your objectives. Never use media for their "bells and whistles" features alone.

7. Tape parts of your lessons if you think the trainee can use the tapes later as a review. Use media to advantage, not simply because they're there.

Presenting Training

The essentials of presentation are content and process. Content includes all the ideas, concepts, information, and skills that will be focused on during instructional and learning time. Process is how you present that content and interact with the trainee. Being able to help your peer trainer fine-tune both content and process techniques is critical to the success of peer training.

Suggest the following guidelines to help your peer trainer to present training:

CONTENT GUIDELINES FOR PEER TRAINERS

1. *Remember to tell the trainee what the objectives are for each lesson.* Plan a lesson for 15 minutes worth of time.

2. *Be sure that you define all terms and acronyms that the trainee might not be familiar with.* Don't make assumptions that the trainee knows what seems obvious to you.

3. *Use a variety of mental structures to explain things— stories, analogies, examples, case studies, equations, diagrams, maps, graphs.* Remember that your trainee needs to have intellectual ways of connecting what's new with what's already part of his experience.

4. *Be logical.* Present information so that the trainee can use what he has just learned as a basis for learning the next lesson. Don't skip around. Make logical transitions.

5. *Give the trainee cues.* Point out the critical steps in a new procedure; differentiate the very important from the not so important. Tell the trainee which features of a model are the significant ones and which ones are generic or common to other models. Help your trainee discriminate and differentiate.

6. *Teach by nonexample too.* Tell or show the trainee what something is as well as what it is not. Help your trainee to fix in his mind the information on which you are focusing by showing him the ways in which alternatives are not acceptable.

7. *Ask the trainee to relate new concepts and procedures to his job.* Help the trainee understand how to apply new learning by asking the trainee to tell you.

8. *When the trainee talks, listen.* You might have to reorganize some content or modify some objectives "on the fly" depending on how your trainee is synthesizing and integrating the information you are teaching. Remember that this person is your peer, and has some good ideas too.

Process Guidelines for Peer Trainers

1. *Give the trainee a chance to tell you what he expects to get out of the training.* Get the trainee to write it down on an index card and tape it to the wall during training. Refer to this statement later during your teaching when the trainee begins to accomplish what he expected to accomplish. Do this early in your peer training to let your trainee know that you will be instrumental in this accomplishment and that you care about the trainee and his learning successes.

2. *Give the trainee a chance to establish his own credibility.* Do this by asking how he got to be where he is now, and discussing how his former positions or schooling will probably play a part in the new position. Generate some enthusiasm for the current training by relating it to the trainee's previous successes.

3. *Be aware of your pace of presentation.* Be ready to adjust it if it seems too fast or too slow, too dull or too animated.

4. *Answer the trainee's questions.*

5. *Give and receive feedback.* Be gracious; remember you're in this together.

6. *Maintain smiling eye contact.*

7. *Use the "mirror" technique if a trainee gives you a wrong response.* Say back to the trainee exactly what he has said, giving the trainee a chance to hear and analyze that response. Preface your mirroring with the statement, "I believe I heard you say. . . ." Follow it up with, "Is this what you meant to say? Have you thought of this other approach?" or "What do you imagine would be the end results if you acted upon this?" Try to let the trainee figure out what was wrong with the response, then identify and list the errors as a review for the trainee. Use errors as an opportunity for good teaching. Never ignore them or make light of them.

8. Give the trainee time to practice new mental or physical skills under your supervision.

Setting Up a Laboratory Session

A lab session is a special kind of training that is often well handled by peer training. There are several variations of lab training. In one kind, a peer trainer works side by side with the trainee, demonstrating, coaching, and giving feedback. In another, the peer trainer sets the rules, assembles the materials, gets the trainee going on his own, and then departs. A third variation is a peer trainer who functions as an individual tutor or troubleshooter on call to a small number of peers engaged in a lab experiment.

As a manager, before you assign someone the task of being a lab session trainer, tutor, or coach, make sure that your prospective trainer:

- Has enough time to allow trainees to engage in trial and error.
- Is thoroughly knowledgeable regarding the consequences of the trainee's experimentation.
- Has the resources to deal with the consequences of the trainee's experimentation.
- Knows how to operate all lab equipment.
- Is patient with learners in a lab.
- Knows about lesson plans, if it is his responsibility to design training, and prepares them adequately prior to lab training.
- Knows the standards or specifications of the products of experimentation and is thoroughly familiar with lab procedures.
- Is willing to help the trainee set up and dismantle equipment used in experiments and to share responsibility for good lab practices regarding safety, order, and cleanliness.

Selected Sample Peer Training

The following section presents five sample peer training situations and lists presentation techniques that are appropriate for each. You can use these lists to help train your peer trainer.

1: New Employee Orientation

A new employee has joined a research and development group in a small company that operates in teams. As a manager, you have assigned one of the team members to be the "big brother" of this new employee and charged him with the job of teaching the new team member "the ropes" during the next two weeks.

This is a situation in which membership in and acceptance by the group are important goals for all new employees. Because it's an R&D group, the new employee has a specific, high-level skill that the company values and needs. Existing team members also have specific, high-level skills. This kind of peer training situation might be replicated in sales training with the hiring of a new sales rep for a specific product line; in the hiring of a new management staff person with specific responsibilities yet a general requirement that she work with the management team; or in a retail operation in which a new buyer has been hired for a specific fashion line yet must operate as part of a team with other buyers of related lines.

Peer trainers in situations like these can usually get right down to the business of orientation because they see no conflict with or challenge to their own security from the "new kid on the block" whose job assignment is clearly in another area of expertise.

These are some basic **presentation techniques** for a sample lesson in this kind of peer training:

Lesson title: Checking Out Lab Equipment

1. Have a copy of the equipment catalog for the trainee to refer to.
2. Explain that the Checkout Center works like a library.
3. Explain the department policy on borrowed lab equipment.
4. On the checkout form, point out the space for item number.
   - Review the six-digit item coding system; suggest paying attention to the last four digits alone (because the first two are a building code of use to Central Services only).
   - Point out some ten of the most frequently borrowed items in this department (highlight the catalog with yellow marker) so that the trainee can anticipate usage and plan her own checkout accordingly.

2: Worker Pool

You run a house painting contracting company. Typically, you have projects going within certain targeted geographic areas, and you assign your pool of workers to a specific geographic area. The seasonal nature of your business is such that work gets "bunched up"—schedules slip, clients have problems or considerations that interfere with completing work as originally planned, or your workers get sick. You have a policy of filling in with a worker of equal competence whenever a worker is temporarily off the job (because of reassignment to cover the schedule better or because of illness or emergency).

This is a situation where peer training works well. Making money in this kind of business depends on communication and cooperation among workers in a worker pool. Peer-to-peer efforts pay off. Other "worker pools" that are equally suited to peer training are insurance clerks, secretarial or word processing pools, customer service telephone reps, programmer pools, and consulting services. Workers in these situations also are often called upon to "cover" for each other for temporary periods.

To do this kind of training, assign each new employee that you hire to a peer trainer for a few hours of basic training in the practices that make your business the best in the area. Build your peer-to-peer communication network as each new hire comes on board.

These are some sample **presentation techniques** for a peer lesson in a worker pool:

Lesson title: First Steps in Taking Over When Another Worker
Is Temporarily Off the Job

1. Give the trainee a list of current projects with the phone number and principal client contact of each.
2. Review the company's policy of providing substitute workers of equal competence within 24 hours.
3. Show the trainee where spare cans of paint are stored and explain the color coding system.
4. Show the trainee where to find the client paperwork and the correct procedures for using it.
   • Don't take anything out of here—use the copy machine

next to the file cabinet if you have to have your own copy.

• Refile papers with the job number always at top right.

5. Show the trainee the difference between job number and invoice number. (There is no need for painters to deal with invoice numbers; job numbers are sufficient.)

6. Show the trainee how to fill out the redeployment card and enter it into the redeployment time clock.

7. Show the trainee how to fill out the personal wage and hours sheet.

3: Specific Procedure

Another kind of peer training that works well is training that is specific to a certain procedure whose guidelines are very clear, and successful execution depends upon following steps in a certain order. A peer who day in and day out performs this procedure is usually the best person to train a newcomer in how to do it.

One example of procedure-specific peer training is teaching a new accounting clerk how to verify the accuracy of payroll forms that employees turn in weekly. Procedure-specific situations are found in most kinds of businesses. Other examples are technical editing procedures, packaging or assembly procedures, personnel interviewing procedures, setting up seminars. Procedure-specific situations range from narrow technical situations to broad human relations situations.

These are some **presentation techniques** for a peer lesson in a procedure-specific situation:

Lesson title: How to Verify the Accuracy of Payroll Forms

1. Organize forms by employee payroll number. The trainee should organize the stack of payroll forms in ascending order by employee payroll number (for example, 123, 124, 125).

2. Verify matrix total. Point out the matrix total. Be sure the trainee knows how to add up the vertical and horizontal cells so that each axis arrives at the same total. Have the trainee do about a dozen actual matrix checks to be sure he gets into the habit of doing this first.

3. Record errors on the inspection error form. Give the trainee the inspection error form. Point out the place to record the employee payroll number and the columns for matrix error and total discrepancy. Guide the trainee while he records the employee payroll number and places a check mark in the "matrix error" column on the inspection error form for several actual cases.

4. Verify totals. Point out the "total" box at the bottom of the payroll form. Guide the trainee through about a dozen employee payroll forms to be sure he cross-checks the matrix total with the total box at the bottom. Show the trainee where to record a discrepancy on the inspection error form (check mark in the "total discrepancy" column.)

5. Establish a work rhythm. Give the trainee some time to practice reading the matrix, verifying the totals, and recording the proper information on the inspection error forms. Watch the trainee for about seven to ten minutes to be sure he is not wasting time by random eye movements over the form. Be sure the trainee focuses first on the matrix and then goes directly to the total box at the bottom.

4: Specific Machine

Peer training works well in a situation where the new employee is required to operate a specific machine in the same way a current employee does. In this situation, the current employee may be the only one who operates this kind of machine, so her expertise is the only in-house expertise you can tap to provide instruction.

Like procedure-specific training, machine-specific training requires a trainer who has the routine of the job well established, and knows on a logical level as well as on a "gut" level what steps to follow if problems arise.

Specific machines can be as common as a new typewriter or as uncommon as a nuclear reactor simulator. The following **presentation techniques** are for part of the startup function of a refinery's binary column.

Lesson title: Overview to Introducing Feed

1. Be sure the trainee can identify and locate all required valves.
2. Be sure the trainee can identify and locate all controllers (pressure, flow, temperature, level).
3. Explain the relationship between level, pressure, temperature, and flow of feedstock.
4. Quiz the trainee on his understanding of these relationships. Be sure it's accurate before going through the procedure for introducing feed. Correct the trainee's misunderstandings.

5: Critical Path

Peer training also works well in a situation where the new employee's job is in the critical path of another current employee's job. In this situation, the current employee knows what it is that the new employee must do to make the work go forward. The outputs of one job are the inputs of another. Peer training in this situation concentrates on these outputs and inputs, not on the details of how to do the "real work" of the new employee's job.

Examples of this kind of situation are computer programming on a large project such as a Department of Defense contract or on a payroll system for a large corporation, growing cultures in a laboratory, factory assembly-line work, team sports such as baseball, or doing a head-to-toe beauty makeover in a beauty salon. All these situations require the outputs of one person's efforts as inputs to another person's work. The peers at this junction can learn from each other in order for work to be productive. One person's work is in the critical path of another's.

The peer trainer might use the following **presentation techniques** in a critical path situation.

Lesson title: Stacking and Transfer

1. Explain to the trainee how your job fits into the big picture of the finished product.
2. Show the trainee your output design specifications for

the clamp he will be taking from you. Point out the spec for the bend (this is what the trainee has to focus on).
3. Discuss with the trainee your typical output speed and daily totals. Be sure the trainee understands how many clamps come through the line every hour and every day.
4. Take the trainee over to the line itself to watch where the outcoming clamps are automatically stacked. Show the trainee how things get fouled up when the bend is not in the right place. Show the trainee how the counter adjusts for rejects, and how to stop the line if any clamp gets jammed.
5. Show the trainee how to record on the PC the hourly input of clamps that he is now responsible for. Read the output counter and forward the stack of usable clamps to his workstation.

In Brief

Peer training can be an important way of transmitting company values from employee to employee and of saving you time and money. Choosing the peer who's right for the job of being an instructor takes discrimination, and training that chosen peer to be an instructor requires some special attention on your part. This chapter has given you some ideas and tools for doing peer training effectively.

The following checklist will help you to choose the right peer trainer and also help your chosen peer trainer to function as an instructor by following some basic instructional techniques.

MANAGER'S CHECKLIST 3

How to Use Peer Training

_____ 1. Choose a competent high performer.
_____ 2. Choose a self-confident person who likes to share ideas and techniques.

_____ 3. Choose someone with patience.

_____ 4. Be sure to allow your peer trainer some flexibility in performing his own job during the time peer training is taking place.

_____ 5. Help your peer trainer to choose a method of presentation that matches the nature of the job. Suggest that the instructional time be as interactive as possible, using a hands-on approach to methods, procedures, and skill development.

_____ 6. Emphasize that peer training should be as professional as classroom instruction; that materials and media have to be of good quality, even for only one trainee.

_____ 7. Encourage the peer trainer to think in terms of 15-minute lessons and to write brief lesson plans.

_____ 8. Help your peer trainer to design checklists and periodic assessment exercises for the trainee.

_____ 9. Suggest that your peer trainer think in terms of presenting content as well as being effective in leading the trainee through the processes that support training—for example, developing expectations, establishing credibility, giving and receiving feedback, correcting errors, and providing practice time.

_____ 10. Make it clear when peer training has ended.

CHAPTER 4

How to Train Groups of Employees

Training a group of employees usually requires running some kind of class. Classroom training has the major advantage of saving you and your company time and money because you as the instructor only have to prepare the lesson once for a number of students.

Teaching a group of adults can be tricky. This chapter outlines some specific group training techniques, and provides guidelines for the use of media, manuals, and handouts. It offers insight into the problems that commonly occur within groups and suggests how to deal with those problems, what to include in an evaluation form, and what you have to know to make a successful presentation. Four sample group situations and the presentation techniques most suitable to each are given at the end of the chapter.

General Characteristics of Groups

When you get a variety of people together in a classroom, they are first and foremost a collection of individuals. But they are also a group, and as a group they take on certain group characteristics; in some classroom situations, these individuals behave as a group rather than as individuals. It's important, therefore, to look at how to do classroom training from the perspective of both the individual and the group.

Who's Who in the Class

Your students will be somewhat alike because of their focus on the same outcome of training—that is, on a new procedure, a new product, a new policy, a new machine, a new business strategy. They will differ, however, in several important ways:

- Even if their jobs are similar, they will learn at different rates and in different styles,
- If their jobs are different, they will each look at what they are learning from the point of view of how they can use it on the job, and their ability to learn will be affected by how practical they believe the training is.
- They will differ according to how they generally operate at work. For instance, some like direction and structure, whereas others prefer consensus and freedom to experiment; some are "groupies" while others are "loners."
- They will differ in how bright they are—how quickly they perceive and respond to stimuli, how accurately they analyze and synthesize data, how quickly and effectively they organize information, how long they can focus before becoming distracted, how well they remember.
- They will also differ according to how they feel—whether tired or wide awake, whether well or contending with a cold, stress, sore back, or stomach ache.

If you decide to take on a group training assignment, think of your group first as a collection of individuals who will probably be more different than alike. Because of this, do yourself a favor and schedule no more than 12 students to a class. Always take some time at the beginning of the training class to go through a "get acquainted" exercise, even if all your trainees know each

other. Ask each trainee in the presence of all the others to
describe in a few words what he or she expects to get out of the
class, and to give some other personal piece of information such
as length of time with the company or other jobs previously
held. Be sure you acknowledge the individuals in your class and
send them the message that you care about how each person
does on the job. Don't treat the group as one big blank face.

What to Expect From the Group

In a classroom, it's harder to get across all of the content
because the processes or group dynamics seem to get in the
way. As the trainer, stay focused on both content and process.
In any kind of training, these are important, but in group training
they take on heightened meaning. Your trainees will contribute
to your ability or inability to deal with both the content of
lessons and the processes that support or undermine your success as a trainer.

Some group members will be ready to solve problems; some
will come enthusiastic to share information; some will act as
helpful coordinators and synthesizers; some will always be
willing to give examples; some will be good at helping you to
motivate and challenge other members of the group; some will
encourage others, but others will be self-centered and obstruc-
tive to the forward movement of the group. In short, each
member of a group generally "marches to a different drummer."

The secret to effective group instruction is to manage the
group's dynamics. Understand the nature of your group, and be
prepared with techniques to move the group forward. Group
psychology begins to take hold as soon as you shut the door of
the classroom. Are you ready?

Successful Group Techniques

Be prepared. Have all your materials in the classroom, organized and ready for trainees to use. Be sure lights, heat, air
conditioning, and machines (projectors, VCRs, tape recorders,

computers) work. Be sure the seats and tables are arranged the way you want them to be. Be sure table tops are clean and no trash is lying around. Be sure you have enough space (for example, an extra table for your slides) so that you can put your teaching materials within easy reach. Be sure you have blackboard space or clean flipchart pages and markers if you need them. Be sure you have course evaluation forms for the trainees to fill out at the end of class.

How to Keep a Group's Attention

The following guidelines will help you keep your trainees' attention during class:

1. Focus the class's attention on yourself from the very beginning. If all the trainees are not from your department, state your name, job title, and work location. Write your business telephone number on the blackboard or flipchart where it can be seen throughout class. If necessary, have the students introduce themselves. Also, provide basic "housekeeping" information (such as where the rest rooms are, where water and coffee can be found, where the lunch room is, where phone calls can be made, where the copy machine is).

2. Tell your students what they will be able to do at the completion of training. State the goal simply and clearly at the beginning of class. Restate it to reestablish your position of authority after the students have had a chance to introduce themselves, and so as to let them hear the goal from your point of view. Be sure to establish yourself as the instructional leader early in the class—your students probably know you only as a work leader. Get their attention now in this new capacity by telling them what you hope they will learn.

3. Learn each student's name. Chances are that you know many of your trainees, but chances are too that you don't know everyone in your class. Figure out how to memorize who's who, perhaps by having your trainess write their first names on large index cards made into "tent" cards placed in front of them.

Have each trainee write on both sides of the tent so that classmates can also see the names. Refer to students by first name at many points during your teaching.

4. Give praise when students do something right. Be sure other students hear you.

5. Keep the pace lively; don't let anyone get lazy or sleepy.

6. Give breaks after hard lessons or long periods of sitting. Reestablish your authority immediately after breaks by moving to the front center of the classroom.

7. Don't lecture for more than ten minutes at a time. Give your students a chance to do exercises, to ask questions, and to interact with each other.

8. Make and remake eye contact with each person in the class.

9. Move around the classroom; don't plant yourself in one spot.

10. Vary the pitch of your voice occasionally. Don't drone.

11. Use humor directed at yourself; share "horror stories" and funny incidents on the job.

12. Repeat important points, writing them down so that your students can see as well as hear key pieces of knowledge. Reinforce learning.

13. Talk in short sentences and use everyday words.

14. Rephrase new technical information in simpler terms by the use of analogies and examples and relate it to specific jobs held by trainees in the class.

15. Use colored markers, slides, transparencies, even music to add variety and another dimension of interest to plain words in print.

16. Don't be afraid to rearrange seats or to break up the group into pairs or small groups of three or four people. Keep the class active, and show that you are in charge.

How to Get Trainees to Participate

Teaching a group of students is a lot more fun and a lot more effective if you encourage participation during lessons. People in groups also tend to feel more responsible for their own and everyone else's learning and to be more committed to action when the group is highly participatory. Creative juices are set flowing and problem-solving behavior is encouraged by the stimulation that active groups provide.

Here are some guidelines for getting your trainees to participate during lessons:

1. Direct questions to specific people by first name early in your teaching and often later on. Smile and keep eye contact with the person to whom you are directing the question. Build up an expectation in other trainees that they will be called on too.

2. Use two basic types of questions—"closed" questions that have yes or no answers, and "open" questions that require a trainee to elaborate or explain. To get the class going, or to encourage a shy person, use the closed type of question first. After the class gets used to the exchange of ideas through questioning, go on to the open questions. Get them warmed up by throwing out an open question for everybody to think about— for example, "Now, how would you tackle that one?" or "Where do you think this point of view originated?" or "How about this as a possibility?"

3. Immediately relate any good idea that a trainee comes up with to his job and to the jobs of others in the class if you can. Build on a trainee's learning by expanding the application of it. This means that you'll have to listen very carefully during the students' introductions of themselves to associate each person with the right job.

4. At transition points between topics, get a trainee to help wrap up the ideas first discussed by telling the class how she can use those ideas on the job. Try to avoid an obvious transition statement such as "That's the end of this section; any questions?" If you do that, chances are that no one will want to say anything. Adults see through "scripts" and they tend to be turned off by them. It's much better to use an exchange of ideas at a point of transition because this helps the trainees integrate the new learning into their own job experiences.

5.   Listen to your students. Don't do all the talking. Discipline yourself to allow them to talk, but don't let them go off on tangents. If you find a particularly knowledgeable student, let that student take over for you for a few minutes.

6. Encourage feedback from your students and accept it graciously, even if it is critical of you or of part of the course. If something you try doesn't work, be ready to scrap it or to try another approach. Remember, you're all adults—they make mistakes sometimes and so do you. Honesty helps encourage participation. Sometimes the class leaps forward in understanding when you all realize that you're in this together, working hard to find solutions to common problems.

7. Give feedback to individual students about how they are performing; let them know the steps they are doing right or wrong, or the skills they are demonstrating well or poorly. Be specific so that they can see what they have to correct in order to do their jobs better.

8. Give the class time to work on problems and to do exercises. Realizing that each learner will approach a problem differently, allow plenty of time to accommodate each person. Before letting the class work on its own, give many different kinds of stimuli. For instance, describe how the finished product will work for those students who need to imagine success; hold up an example of a correctly completed form for those students who need a graphic example to follow; give clues about key processes for those students who like to solve puzzles; or tell a story about someone who ran into trouble because he didn't use this process or product. As you prepare your lessons, think about many different ways of presenting ideas in order to appeal to and encourage the many different styles of learners in your classroom.

9. Get close to your students. Walk around the room, look over their shoulders, sit beside them, have them help you at the flipchart. Watch your body language—don't fold your arms in front of you, rattle change in your pocket, or play with your jewelry. Wear "easy" clothing; unbutton your suit jacket. Be, and give the appearance of being, comfortable yet professional.

10. If you use handouts and student manuals, refer to them often and encourage the students to follow along. Use a handout

to "talk" the student through an example or as a guide for self-study or class exercises. Get students involved, with guidance, in the materials of the course. If you use reference materials, show the students how to use them. Point out the "good stuff."

11. Never put down or embarrass a student. Find something good about that person and focus on that. A slow or inexperienced employee has had many successes in learning and in work too, and will learn better in your class if you can begin to relate the new knowledge to those past successes.

12. Always think in terms of alternatives to lecturing. Lecturing absolutely discourages participation. Breaking up a class into smaller groups encourages participation. Seat groups of four people around tables instead of having the whole class strung out in rows. If you have to sit theater style, have members of the class sit in pairs, with an empty seat between each pair. Break up the tendency of people to be inert by structuring their seating in ways that encourage interaction.

13. If you use flipcharts or a board, get trainees to help you. Get them involved in using these instructional tools, have them elaborate or explain what you've just said, or get them to record information gathered during small group work.

How to Use Manuals and Handouts

Manuals and handouts are tools. Like all good tools, they have to feel right in the hand of the user and they have to fit the job to be done. They should be attractive and easy to use. Don't be tempted to put everything you can think of into a manual or packet of handouts. Trainees don't want to bother to read a lot of extraneous information, and you don't want to tempt them into throwing it all in the trash. Manuals and handouts should be spare and directly to the point—useful and appropriate tools for learning.

When you use manuals and handouts during lessons, be specific about what you are referring to, and give the trainees enough time to find their places, ask questions, and take notes. Don't make using the manual a burden. Suggest how it can be helpful to them back on the job as a reminder of training or as a source of important information.

The following information will be helpful if you have to design your own trainee manual. It suggests the minimum you must do to create a useful tool for your trainees. If you're lucky, you'll be able to use a training manual that's already in existence. In that case, all you'll need to do is check through it for proper sequence and possibly dated material in case you need to alert students to problem areas.

Basics of Designing Your Own Trainee Manual

1. *Keep it simple but classy.* The two simplest trainee manuals are (1) a copy of your content outline, or (2) a paper copy of your overhead transparencies or slides. Another possibility is a combination of these. Use good paper, be sure the printing and copying are dark and legible, attach a cover page with the company logo, course title, date, place of training, and your name and telephone number.

2. *Don't crowd the pages.* Leave plenty of white space around words so that trainees can make notes.

3. *Make it useful.* If your course teaches how to do a new procedure (for example, taking inventory, ordering merchandise, making telephone followups, recording customer complaints, operating a new machine, doing paperwork after a sales call), you might want to make your trainee manual a set of lists of the steps involved and a paragraph or two explaining why each list is important. Staple the lists together for the trainee to refer to during training and later on the job.

4. *Label accurately.* It's a good idea to let a colleague—perhaps another manager—review your manual for consistency and accuracy before you reproduce it for trainees. When you've been in a job for awhile, you get used to nicknaming parts and processes or to using acronyms in everyday discussions. Your trainees might not understand your abbreviated language. Be sure that all diagrams are accurately labeled and that you are consistent throughout the manual.

Using Handouts Effectively

Handouts are usually copies of course-related information that has appeared in the form of newspaper or magazine articles, memos, organization charts, company policy statements, research reports, pictures of product lines, or tables and charts. Handouts are important but independent materials; that is, they are not part of the essential written material of the course.

Handouts should be complete and legible. Be sure when you copy a magazine article, for example, that you incorporate the magazine title and issue date. If you have to reduce a chart or table to get it on your paper, be sure that you do get it all and that it is readable in reduced size. Be sure copied materials are copied straight on the page. Do a test run of each handout before duplicating a dozen copies of each so that you can check the quality of the reproduction.

Using handouts requires some preplanning and setting up so that the "stage business" doesn't get in the way. Keep a stack of each type of handout on your instructor's table, and pass out each one at the appropriate time in the lesson. Don't hand them all out at once, making the trainee shuffle through a pile of paper.

You can sometimes use handouts as a crutch for those times when your voice is giving out or you just can't stand to be on your feet one more minute. You can use a handout as an assignment, asking the class to take 15 minutes to read an article (while you sit down) and to think about the relevant points in relation to their jobs or to the afternoon's proposed workshop session. You can use a handout of a chart to give a student the opportunity to take over the class for a few minutes and to explain it to the class while you go down the hall to the vending machine.

You can use handouts as vehicles for breaking up into small groups, giving each group a different handout to analyze and to report back on to the whole group later. A procedural-type handout can be given to a group facilitator or leader whom you designate to lead each small group through a problem identification session.

The secret to successful use of handouts is to use them as

stand-alone documents that are introduced at meaningful points in a lesson to enhance or change its direction. Always make them attractive and easy to use.

How to Use Media

Chapter 3 explains the use of audiovisual media in peer training. These media are even more helpful during classroom instruction because they provide variety. The added stimuli of sight, sound, color, and motion appeal to students in various ways, helping to motivate them and to clarify the concepts you are teaching. Remember that media support instruction, never replace it. Don't be tempted to show a film just to fill up some time or even because it's a great film. Use media to energize your class, to prod the students into thinking in new ways, to illustrate procedures or highlight features of products, and to review or provide background information. Always guide a discussion after a slide series, videotape, or film; never just "let it hang." Before choosing media, ask yourself if this item (film, video, slide) really will do what you want it to and whether it truly fits in with your objective for the lesson.

Here are seven guidelines to consider when using media:

1. *Give your class an idea of what's coming in a video or film.* Help the trainees organize their thoughts ahead of time so that they can view and listen to the media presentation with some structure and sense of relevance to their jobs. Tell them several things to watch for as they interact with media. Never give them the idea that the media presentation is unrelated to the course.

2. *If you use flipcharts, be sure that you practice managing them.* Go through the part of a lesson in which you intend to work at the flipchart in front of a "fake" student (your spouse, a friend). Ask that person to tell you whether your handwriting is readable from a distance, whether you block the student's view when you write, and whether you seem at ease using it. Practice flipping the large sheets of paper. Practice using the

markers you intend to use during class; they sometimes bleed through to the next sheet of paper, and, if this happens, you'll have to plan to write on every other sheet or get new nonbleeding markers. If you plan to post sheets on the walls of the classroom, be sure your tape or pins won't mar the wall finish. Be sure markers don't bleed through to the wall.

3. *Be sure you know how to operate all machines you intend to use.* Be sure you know where to get extra projector bulbs (borrow an extra from your stockroom or A/V room if you can during class). Securely fasten long projector cords to the floor with wide tape so that people don't trip over them. Practice talking and operating a projector at the same time; it is not as easy as it looks. Decide how to refer to images projected on the screen—by using a pencil, a large pointer, an outstretched arm. Decide if you want to stay close to the projector or to the screen while the media show is progressing. Practice doing what you plan to do so you don't appear awkward in front of the class. Don't use any equipment you're not comfortable with; practice to a comfort level or think of a way around using that equipment.

4. *Be sure you check projected images for clarity even from the back of the classroom.* If you handwrite your own transparencies, be sure that your letters are large enough and thick enough to be read from a distance. Don't clutter the page with either words or messages. Be guided by the rule of seven—no more than seven messages, seven listed items, or seven lines per page projected on a screen. Fewer is better; three items are often suggested as the ideal number of items/ideas per page. Generally, people can't comprehend more than seven items at one time.

5. *Use your PC whenever you can to generate well-spaced, graphically pleasing visuals.* If you don't already have some graphics software in your company, consider getting some and using it to make training materials.

6. *Preview any purchased or borrowed videos, films, or slides for relevance to and culture-compatibility with your particular class.* Don't be caught in the middle of your presentation during class with an outdated, erroneous, or sexist image, or with a perspective that might have been appropriate for a developing

company but not for yours. Don't take anyone else's word; preview the entire presentation to see for yourself what its merits are before showing it to students.

7. *Stick to your planned time limit for using media.* Especially when you show a video or set of slides that can be stopped along the way as student questions arise, it's a good idea to allow the media presentation to become interactive, but you'll have to monitor the expenditure of time carefully when it does. It's better to plan ahead for such interaction and to show fewer slides or shorter videos than to have to scrap portions of your presentation because of time overruns. Again, think small. Media support instruction; they do not supplant it. You can get a lot of mileage out of two or three slides per 15-minute period of time.

Problem Groups

In group training, you always run the risk that "groupthink" will take over. When this happens, the psychology of the pack takes precedence over individual expression. Worst-case scenarios include self-centered group members who take the leadership away from you and bring the group along with them; arguments between members of the group that escalate into time-consuming conflicts and cause group members to take sides; groups that can't do the exercises you have assigned and in consequence become agitated and frustrated; individuals who seek attention and cause others in the group to seek attention too; bad jokes, horseplay, or flippant behavior; and groups that decide to leave early before training is finished.

Groups that behave badly tend to affect individual group members in three negative ways: (1) They may force individuals to cling to a convenient group member to weather the storm with, and thus bring about a mutual dependence instead of the independent and supportive behavior that is desired; (2) they encourage individuals to withdraw, to clam up and stop participating and learning while the group war is raging; and (3) they often shoot down individuals who try to rise above the calamity and fight the trend.

Most group problems can either be prevented or readily solved if caught in the early stages. The following sections contain some guidelines for preventing and handling problem groups.

Helpful Hints for Staying Out of Trouble

1. *Be sure that the training goal is enough of a challenge to the group.* Be sure all group members agree that it is the right goal. This means that you'll have to know your training outline so well that you can modify it on the spot if you need to, creating exercises that are more difficult than the ones you originally planned or adding concepts that are more challenging. This means that you'll have to listen very carefully during student introductions when each trainee tells you what he or she expects to get out of the training. You may have to make the training more challenging for only one or two of the class members. Be so thoroughly prepared that you can do this.

2. *Remove any fear of punishment for doing poorly in training.* Be sure an atmosphere of learning and intellectual experimentation is created prior to and during the training.

3. *Be sure training begins at the right mental level for the group.* No one wants to be embarrassed or to look "dumb." Be sure group members have the necessary prerequisites for the training. If they don't, wait until they do or change the level of the training.

4. *Maintain an attitude of facilitating.* Help your trainees to learn. Respect them as experienced adults, competent in many areas of life. Don't let your position as manager get in the way. Think of yourself as managing learning or as positioning each trainee for a certain outcome of training. Be confident in your trainees, and be patient.

How Facilitative Group Leaders Prevent Problems

Facilitative group leaders act to assist the group in accomplishing its tasks, and constantly and deliberately do certain things to maintain and encourage good group dynamics.

The following behaviors are typical of good group leaders. They are separated here into (1) task behaviors and (2) process behaviors.

In terms of *task behaviors,* a good group leader:

- Suggests new ways of looking at a problem if the group gets stuck. This is not intended to solve the problem for the group; instead it opens the group's thinking to other possibilities.
- Fills in an information gap when the group lacks certain requisite data.
- Evaluates or makes a judgment when the group needs an opinion.
- Coaxes or prods a group into a decision if the group is close to one and if it's the right decision.
- Refocuses the group and pulls it all together when it needs help synthesizing or analyzing information.
- Coordinates various group activities so that it stays organized and focused on its task(s).
- Seizes the opportunity for making allies. It is important to take every opportunity to build upon the correct actions or excellent ideas of specific group members. This moves the task forward by giving visibility to exceptional trainees.

In terms of the *group process,* a good group leader:

- Uses active silence. It is important to be an attentive audience to and observer of the group at work. A good group leader never turns off.
- Directs traffic. People must be kept moving in the right direction by putting group members in key positions to improve communication and the flow of task-related activities.
- Mediates differences between group members.
- Provides feedback. A leader must describe actions or present states to the group members involved in order to clarify what's going on.
- Encourages and accepts contributions from the group.

Dealing With Stalled Groups

In spite of your best efforts at preventing group problems, they sometimes happen. The following eight problems are common to groups that have come to a grinding halt. When they occur, here's how to begin to solve them:

1. If the group is dull and passive, use physical movement to create some action. Change places—move purposively from one part of the room to another; think of a reason to gesture dramatically. Move them—rearrange chairs in a circle, regroup around tables; deliberately force some other dynamics to get started.

2. If the group is bored, introduce a new piece of data. Challenge your students with a choice tidbit; make them think you're letting them in on something; tantalize them with having to see their jobs or this training in a new light because of this new data. Prod their mental processes to integrate this new data. Keep your comments focused on data, not information. That is, don't tell them everything they need to know about your choice tidbit; force them into figuring out the relationships.

3. If the group nitpicks and loses sight of the big picture, focus on the uses of training. Suggest that your students remember what created the need for this training in the first place, and tell them exactly how their new skills or knowledge will be applied to fixing that problem. Make them mentally leap beyond the present.

4. If the group has been functioning pretty well, but one person does something to make the group clam up, restate the objectives of training, starting with the very first hour. Go so far as to write these on the blackboard or flipchart. Keep eye contact with one or two trainees you think are fence-sitters, that is, students who could be your allies. Ask these trainees in a nonthreatening way at the appropriate time in your review of objectives whether they agree with you and if they feel they have learned these things earlier. Don't focus on the persons who precipitated the clam-up; skip over them as you try to establish eye contact with other trainees. If you're doing pretty

well with the eye contact, go one step further and ask for an informal vote by show of hands: "How many think you learned this one adequately?" "What about this one?" Get them to reestablish a pattern of independent thinking. Work on individuals through the objectives for training. Go around the room several times if you have to, trying to get eye contact. Encourage the "good guys" with something like, "Great, Lisa. Glad you did. Keep up the good work."

5. If the small groups you've broken into aren't working, regroup. One way to do this is to set up a "fishbowl" in which the best-functioning small group (or a new small group that you appoint) goes about the task, surrounded by everyone else watching silently. Restructure your original number of small groups into just two groups, the doer group and the observer group. You still end up with an active small group, the observers may learn something about how to work better in a small group, and you've minimized your losses. Another approach is to regroup into small groups according to a game plan totally different from the one you started with; for example, instead of grouping people by work assignment, group them by zodiac sign or shoe size. Change the dynamics.

6. If one group member sets a bad example that others are likely to follow, give that person immediate feedback focused only on his bad behavior. For example, if someone stayed out well beyond the limit for coffee break, confront that person immediately with feedback such as "Jack, you're ten minutes late. We'd like to keep coffee breaks to 15 minutes so we can all move forward together." Don't give a bad trend a chance to get started by ignoring what might be ringleader behavior.

7. If group members are getting a little defensive and argumentative toward you, put on the brakes—don't ignore what is happening but rather stop teaching and give them a mirror image of themselves. Say something like "Wait a minute. I observe at this very moment that we seem to be feeling. . . ." Nip it in the bud. Most people will back off when they realize they might be headed for a collision.

8. If the group is noisy and out of control, stop and shift gears. Force a change of focus. Give an assignment, one that

each person has to do individually. Hold up your hands in a "time out" position. Say something like this: "Whoa. Time out. Shift gears. Take out a piece of paper and pencil. List four things that contribute to. . . ." Relate the assignment to the next part of the course, and tell them that.

Handling Killer Comments

You've heard them in meetings, in hallways, rest rooms, lunch-rooms, golf courses, and in the local after-hours gathering spot. They are killer comments, those intentional or unintentional remarks that people make about new ideas. Killer comments can undermine the progress of the group.

Killer comments also surface during training classes because, by nature, training classes are breeding grounds for new ideas. Killer comments can come up during question and answer periods, at feedback times, in small group sessions, or at break times or gathering times before instruction begins. The wise instructor will be alert to killer comments and use them as opportunities to turn the discussion around and counteract the potential negative fallout from such remarks.

The trainer's job is to help strengthen the class's abilities in analyzing information, in considering other points of view, in realizing new relationships, in making informed decisions, and in exercising good judgment. Killer comments are generally an indication that the person making the comment is on the brink of a new discovery or is about to exercise a new skill. Killer comments often serve as a shield to protect the commenter from taking a vulnerable and risky position. The trainer's job is to protect that risk-taker during class. The killer comment often turns out to be the white flag of surrender of a former belief, a signal that learning is about to take place. Your trick is to recognize the signal, to be unwilling to accept the killer comment as the negative it appears to be, and to help the person who made the comment to become more open.

This may mean you'll have to directly stop the killer comment with a statement like "But have you thought about what would happen if . . ." or "Give me three concrete reasons why this seems to be true.'' Whenever you cut a trainee off, or whenever you engineer the situation so that someone else cuts that trainee off, it's your responsibility to your trainee to get right back in there with some assurance and support. Your supportive comments will help the commenter to stay in the discussion and perhaps diverge from the original statements, and you won't let the rest of the group take the killer comment at face value. Support your killer commenter with statements such as: ''I see where you're coming from'' or ''I know you've had a lot of experience with that'' or ''Yes, I do remember when you got a raw deal over a similar situation'' or ''I appreciate your point of view, Woody.''

These killer comments are the ones to watch out for:

It won't work.
We've never done it like that before.
We've tried that a hundred times.
Not practical.
All form and no substance.
Too modern.
Too old-fashioned.
Too expensive.
Too small.
Too big.
Too fast.
Too slow.
It's not in the budget.
We'll never sell it to management.
Too political.
Not political enough.
I don't see the connection.
That's not our responsibility.
Yes, but. . . .

Managing Conflict

Instructors of groups of employees can expect conflict. Conflict is a natural characteristic of groups that are in the process of "forming." A class is one example of a forming group. Conflict itself won't get you into trouble; poor management of conflict will.

Conflict is natural to the period of confronting problems after a class has gone through an orientation period of relative cohesiveness. At a time of conflict, individuals' values, beliefs, experiences, and ego needs clash with each other and have to be reconciled with the developing group norms. Conflict causes people to take sides and to confirm their positions. Conflict is often present when new skills and new ideas have to be learned. It is more apparent in group training than in other kinds of training.

Effective conflict management requires that you do two things: (1) Recognize the validity of each side and (2) provide structure to both sides so that they can maintain a working relationship between themselves. Adversaries are actually mutually dependent on each other; each gives the other fuel for the fires. Like fire, conflict rages on until it is stopped.

One of the quickest ways out of conflict is to hold up the prospect of something new, totally different from the object of the conflict. Parties in conflict will generally agree to yield their ground if they can be made to see that the new idea is worth working for. Compromise implies that each side gives up something for the common good, but this often results in smoking embers that flare up again into major battles. Don't think in terms of compromise; think instead in terms of contributing to something new. Manage the natural conflict phase of group function this way, and thereby move forward with new energy, new commitments, and possibly new solutions. Set up win/win situations.

Other techniques can be used to get all points of view out in the open and to get individuals communicating with each other. Use index cards or the flipchart to solicit and record each person's point of view. Limit each statement to two minutes of time or to a quarter of a flipchart sheet. Structure the responses so that everyone has an equal chance at visibility. Lead a brainstorming discussion in which all points of view are heard, judgment is forbidden, and no one is allowed to ignore or belittle another's ideas. Record the discussion faithfully where all can see. Force the discussion onward until each member of the group has had a chance to speak for about the same length of time. Often the things that bother people lead to new ideas. Make up rules to govern communication and feedback and state them clearly so that you can lead the class back into cohesion and problem resolution.

Making Effective Presentations

There are some special responsibilities attached to being an instructor that are heightened during classroom or group training. It's especially important that you differentiate them in your mind so that you can exercise them independently at different times during lessons as the need arises. These responsibilities have more to do with managing learning than with managing a group of people. They sometimes have to be carried out simultaneously because each trainee is different and brings a different background of experience and a different learning style to class. If you can differentiate them, you can use them on the right people at the right time with a little practice. Learning is usually a reciprocal deal between instructor and student. The basic instructional strategies for teaching one-to-one, found in Chapter 2, suggested ways of helping a single trainee to learn.

Your Responsibilities as an Instructor

The instructional responsibilities outlined below revisit some of those fundamentals, but with a group audience as the target.

1. *Help the trainee to get ready to learn.* Each task or objective for each lesson requires a short period of getting ready. This can take only a few seconds, and can be as simple as your saying to the group "Okay now, be ready to listen for the beep" or "Remember the three things we learned this morning about pulse rate." If a trainee or two is still wandering, repeat or paraphrase the statement using his or her name in it: "Jeffrey,

be ready to listen for the beep'' or ''Carla, get ready to take Bob's pulse.''

2. *Tell the students what you expect them to learn during training.* This gives individual class members a chance to organize their own experience relative to that expectation and to do a quick check of where they must pay special attention. Give the class a chance to respond to your statement of objectives so that you can be sure you're all together right from the beginning. Be ready to make adjustments if you have pitched the material at too high or too low a level.

3. *Know the difference between description and explanation.* Use each at the right time. Description is the most basic kind of information. It includes labeling, defining, or pointing out the features of something. Start with description. Explanation is more advanced than description. After you finish describing something, stop and then go on to explaining it. Don't mix up the two processes because most trainees can't handle both together, especially when your lessons involve new ideas or new skills. Explaining involves telling why something is important, how it works, how it might be used on the job, and often uses relationships such as analogies, formulas, diagrams, and examples. Mixing description and explanation leads to frustration and to a split between those who got it and those who didn't. Be sure everyone understands all the descriptive information before you begin explaining. This is sometimes hard to do because you know what you're talking about in an integrated sort of way. Whenever you introduce new information, separate the descriptive from the explanatory.

4. *Present every step or procedure simply.* Tell them what to do. Don't mix in explanation with the steps. Write out the steps in very simple language beginning with an action word. These are examples: ''Find the balance''; ''transfer the six-digit number to the box at the bottom of the page''; ''choose a color''; ''read the last paragraph''; ''bend your knees, keeping your back straight.'' Number steps in the order in which they must be performed. Be very clear and make sure you use words consistently. Stop after four or five steps to be sure that everyone understands. Take it slow and keep it simple. Give group

members a chance to get their heads organized. Some will want to memorize the steps as you go along; some may want to write them down; others will be imagining how to do each step. The characteristic reactions of trainees do take time, and in a group they take more time.

5. *Give cues*. Do this for the class as a whole and for individuals who need extra help. Cues can be of two kinds: some may just give that extra little push when students are about ready to act; others can be related to an individual trainee's experience. These are examples: "When the color turns blue," "watch the temperature," and "listen for two responses"; or "think about your total for last week," "remember Chicago," "consider Eric's conclusion."

6. *Provide supervised practice*. Give your students time to practice and to demonstrate to you that they have learned. Don't leave them during exercises or practice time. Be available and visible as a coach or information source. Guide them into getting ready to apply what they have learned back on the job. Move around the room; each person will require some individual attention. It's okay to generate some chaos, action, noise, or jumping up for coffee during practice time. Control the class through your role as the expert mentor during this period. Set a limit on practice time. Get around to each class member quickly at the beginning of practice time, then return to anyone who needs extra help.

7. *Give specific and meaningful feedback often*. Give it to the class as a whole as well as to individuals. Give praise when it is deserved, and give information that will help individuals to correct their mistakes. Use feedback in a group situation to encourage not only the person to whom it is directed but also other trainees who are likely to respond to your feedback comments.

Creating Lesson Plans

Your general approach to creating lesson plans should be to think of each lesson as a way of drawing out of people what is logical or commonsensical rather than as a way of implanting information in them. In preparing your lessons, keep what your students will be able to do at the forefront of your thinking. List one or two objectives for the trainee for each 15-minute segment of teaching. Follow the lesson plan format presented in Chapter 2 of this book. Put groups of lessons together to form a topic.

The following 12-step procedure will help you to create individual lessons:

1. Identify a topic and give it a short title.

2. Assemble all the materials that are related to this topic, for example, user manuals, memos, charts, journal articles, case studies, success stories, models.

3. Figure out what you want the trainee to be able to do regarding this topic. Think small. Turn this trainee action into one or two objectives for each 15-minute period of instruction. Write the objectives for each 15-minute segment on a separate piece of paper. (You'll probably have several pages for each topic.)

4. Arrange and number the pages of objectives in the order in which you plan to teach them.

5. Look at the objectives to see if each one can be measured and then determine how you will get your trainees to show you that they have learned each one. Consider informal question-and-answer sessions, exercises, and individual problem solving; work at the blackboard, using new information in an old formula, and demonstrating how to do it. Make a notation regarding measurement next to each objective if you think you won't remember.

6. Sort through your assembled materials and decide what you'll need to accomplish each page of objectives. Count on about four major areas of content based on your assembled materials for each page of objectives. Make a content outline of these major areas on each page of objectives.

7. Decide if any of your materials should be reproduced and handed out to students. Put them in a separate folder or pile so that you will remember to do the copying ahead of time.

8. Decide if there are any prerequisites for this topic, based on the objectives you have set and the content you plan to cover.

9. Choose the most appropriate instructional method for this topic. Expand your thinking to include such options as small discussion groups, small problem-solving groups, demonstrations, role playing, field trips, workshops, case studies, video critiques, and the making of a videotape.

10. List the media or audiovisual aids that you'll need for each lesson.

11. Write the lesson plans for this topic in lesson plan format. Reread your objectives and content outlines to simplify and refine; omit words, make them briefer, choose words more carefully, put the action words first. Set yourself up with as spare a set of lessons as you can manage. (You'll appreciate the extra effort expended on this when you are "on stage" during class and have time only for a quick glance at your lesson plans.)

12. Start all over again with step 1 for each new topic of your course.

Your Instructor's Guide

The simplest complete instructor's guide is a set of lesson plans stapled together according to topics. There are, of course, variations on this such as lesson plans on the right-hand page and notes to yourself on the corresponding left-hand page, or lesson plans on the right-hand page and a script on the left-hand page. Some experienced instructors simply teach from a list of objectives or from a paper copy of their slides.

Do yourself a favor as a beginning instructor by working from lesson plans grouped together as topics. In order to see the words more clearly in a classroom situation, print the objectives and content outlines in bold type. Leave plenty of white space around words, and make wide margins.

Plan 15-minute instructional periods, but in a classroom situation allow for 20 minutes to accomplish what you have designated as a 15-minute segment. This allows you some extra time to deal with the group dynamics that are always a part of teaching groups of employees.

Follow the lesson plan format given in Chapter 2. Give each lesson a title (which may be the same as the topic, but may differ to reflect the objective), state its purpose in a few words, list the materials you'll have to have on hand for this lesson, state your one or two behavioral objectives for this lesson, and include just enough of a content outline to keep yourself on track during this lesson.

Put a cover page on the set of topics that will include the title you give to this course, the date and place it will be delivered, and your name as the instructor. You'd be surprised how quickly you can forget when training occurred and what you did, and how often you may wish you could remember. A simple instructor guide can be used again and again. Do it right the first time and you won't be sorry.

Balancing Each Lesson

Plan to balance each 15-minute lesson with comments and actions that explain, that get trainees involved in trying out new ideas and skills, and that give trainees a chance to know how they're doing. Explaining and experimenting should take up about 80 percent of your instructional time; feedback and evaluation should take up no more than 20 percent. The explaining usually comes easily; concentrate in your preparation on the experimenting or hands-on part of each lesson, which is equally important. Remember, you're teaching adults, and they need the chance to make it real. They have little tolerance for theory only. Adults don't need to be tested and graded, but they do need frequent expressions of approval or correction. Feedback tends to motivate adults to keep going. Effective presentation will exhibit a balance between explanation, experimentation, and evaluation.

Feedback and Evaluation

Giving feedback to trainees is sometimes hard to do. Managers often have an easier time with this than do nonmanagerial instructors because of their previous experience in giving feedback to employees during performance reviews and salary discussions. The rules are basically the same in both situations. Essentially, be quick and be specific. Don't wait until the end of training to tell someone that she was terrific, or that he still has a long way to go. That kind of late, unspecific feedback is not helpful either as a motivator or as a trigger for corrective action during learning.

The following guidelines will help you to give feedback:

1. Address the trainee by his first name. Establish eye contact and smile when you say the person's name.
2. Tell the person what you observed her doing. Use the word "I" in your statement. Say, "I noticed that you. . . ." or "I observed that you. . . ." or "I saw that you. . . ." Referring to yourself first softens the blow if it's a suggestion for correction; if you say "You did. . . ." first, it comes across as an accusation.
3. Describe the effect of what the person did or said on the group, on another person, or on the product or work operation.
4. Don't overload the circuits. Don't press on and on with either positive or negative comments. Adults rebel at being put on the spot in front of their peers.
5. Don't hit and run. Give the person a chance to assimilate the feedback and respond to you. Stay focused on the specific action you observed. Steer the question-and-answer discussion around to the reason for the feedback. Keep it behavioral; don't get into personalities.

Group presentations usually benefit from trainee evaluations of the course. For the trainees, taking a few minutes at the end of the course to integrate what was learned in response to a structured evaluation form can be helpful to the learning process, to their ability to transfer that learning to the job, and to their overall sense of satisfaction. For the instructor, the results of the evaluation are useful as input for improving the course the next time around.

The evaluation questions don't have to be elaborate or lengthy. Choose or create a trainee evaluation form that can be presented on one page. If you use one already in existence, be sure you update it for this particular course. Read it carefully; don't automatically assume that it will be right for the course you have given.

When you design an evaluation form, don't just go for a "smiles test" or seek a pat on the back. Ask specific questions that get to the heart of how you designed this training experience. Always give the trainee space in which to write additional comments (the back of the form is okay). Ask the trainee to elaborate when pointing to problem areas. Don't expect 100 percent cooperation in this exercise. About 10 percent of a typical class will not want to fill out an evaluation form. Make it clear that doing so is optional, but will be very much appreciated. Remind trainees that they need not put their names on the paper.

These are some of the categories and specific questions that you might include on your evaluation form:

OBJECTIVES

- Too hard, too easy, just right?
- Expressed clearly?
- Organized to encourage learning?

CONTENT

- All relevant to the job?
- Anything seem to be missing?
- Organized right?
- Explained thoroughly?

COURSE SETTING

- Conducive to learning?
- Equipment working?
- Room comfortable?
- Materials of good quality?

INSTRUCTOR'S PRESENTATION

- Clear?
- Relevant to individual class members?
- Relevant to your own situation?

- What percentage of training was relevant to your job?
- How soon do you intend to use what you learned in this class?
- How confident are you about going back and trying it?
- How much money/time do you think you can save by using these new skills/knowledge on your job?

Selected Sample Group Training

This section presents four different group training situations, and suggests presentation techniques that will work for each. The advantages of this kind of group training are then listed for each selected sample.

1: The Case Study
The Clean Room Assembly Worker

Marge works in an electronics assembly plant. Her job is to mount the chip containing the integrated circuit onto a board. She has to do this to a gross and a half of boards during her eight-hour shift. This particular day, the glue machine gets jammed. This doesn't happen, however, until about half a gross of boards have been partially glued. Marge is responsible for the machines she uses and for reaching her daily quota. What does she do now? What does she do to prevent this situation from recurring?

SUGGESTED PRESENTATION TECHNIQUES FOR CASE STUDY

1. Tell trainees why you chose this case. What's the objective?
2. Break the case study time into two parts: one to analyze the current situation and to define all the parts of the current problem, and the other to analyze the desired situation and to define all parts of the solution. Allow enough time. Don't rush the reading time.

3. Provide each trainee with a copy of the case and the two questions to be addressed during training.
4. Suggest what some of the problems might be, but not all of them. Give trainees a few cues as they begin their analyses. Suggest that they make a list of the problems as they read through the case so that later they can come up with solutions.
5. Review the major events and describe the major personalities in the case. Provide descriptions only, not explanations.
6. Either break the class into small groups, each to work on the answers, or treat the class as one group. If you choose small groups, be sure each group has a leader and a recorder. If you choose to treat trainees as one group with yourself as the leader, choose someone to be your recorder.
7. Give the class a few ground rules regarding group problem solving. Accept all comments as valid, record accurately and don't paraphrase, and involve everyone in the discussion.
8. Summarize and conclude the case study by asking trainees how they can apply what they have learned from it to their own jobs.

ADVANTAGES

1. Encourages development of analytical skills and problem-solving behavior.
2. Allows both independent work and group work.
3. Is interesting because trainees feel that they're getting the inside scoop on a business situation or problem.
4. Is relevant because problems that are highlighted in case studies are usually true-to-life job situations.
5. Appeals to trainees who like to read as well as to trainees who like to talk.
6. Gives the instructor some free time for sitting down and observing trainees (when the group is broken into small problem-solving groups).

2: Role Play

You have a classroom full of employees who are training to be salespersons. You use role play as a training technique. The situation is this. Eric has been a customer service representative. His job has changed to that of a salesperson because his company has just begun a major initiative to get more experienced employees out in the field selling company products. He needs to learn the essentials of doing a sales call: (1) how to probe to clarify a potential customer's needs, (2) how to put himself in the customer's position and show empathy, (3) how to demonstrate that his product will meet the customer's needs, and (4) how to close the sale.

SUGGESTED PRESENTATION TECHNIQUES FOR ROLE PLAY

1. Give trainees the facts about Eric. Tell them, write the facts on the blackboard or flipchart, or use a handout called "Role Play Fact Sheet."
2. Make up some typical potential customers. Give trainees the facts about each potential customer. Add these to the "Role Play Fact Sheet."
3. Give trainees the four items, "Essentials of Doing a Sales Call," so that they know what skills they're aiming for in the role plays. Tell them to work to accomplish each of these skills during the role play. (The objectives of training should be obvious during role play.)
4. Pair off the trainees so that half the class becomes Eric and the other half becomes a potential customer. Choose either to have the whole class doing role plays at the same time (very active and noisy, works well in a large group) or have one pair at a time do the role play in front of everyone else (less active, works well in a smaller group).
5. Give the class some choice as to which person they want to be, Eric or the potential customer. Reverse roles later if you have time.
6. Allow time to pull together all the awareness that has developed among the role players. Use a "debriefing"

exercise in which trainees can tell you what they have learned about the four essential skills. Tabulate their comments in some organized way on the blackboard or flipchart. Give trainees time to take notes; don't erase helpful suggestions or flip the flipchart pages too fast.

ADVANTAGES

1. Trainees are active during role play either as actors or as observers. They don't get bored during role play.
2. Playing out roles can demonstrate many solutions to problems.
3. Role play can lead to increased self-confidence.
4. Role play is a "safe" way to examine attitudes, beliefs, and feelings. Trainees are not usually defensive or threatened when they are playing a role.
5. Role play suggests analogies to current problems. The similarity of problems and solutions can encourage similar action back on the job.
6. Role play is usually fun.

3: Lecture

Your lecture is entitled "Safe Practices While Working at a Visual Display Terminal (VDT)," and you synthesize its contents at the beginning by saying: "This lecture will alert you to the issues connected with and the practices recommended for the safe use of visual display terminals. Safe practices have to do with the equipment itself and the work area in which it is installed. The important foci of safe practices include your chair, your desk, the screen, the keyboard, lighting, documents, and the time you spend in a working position in front of your VDT.

"In this lecture, we will consider radiation safety issues, the psychological and human factors in VDT use, federal and state legislation regarding VDT use, management trends, training, labor contracts, and labor practices regarding VDT use."

SUGGESTED PRESENTATION TECHNIQUES FOR THE LECTURE

1. Define terms and acronyms early in the lecture. Use slides or overhead transparencies for this purpose so that trainees can hear and see the definitions.
2. Document your lecture either by writing it all out, double- or triple-spaced so it's easy to read, or by putting it in outline form on index cards. Or, plan to lecture directly from your slides or transparencies, using them as your outline.
3. Highlight key points by using a highlighter pen on paper copies of your lecture or by making marginal notes on your slides or transparencies.
4. Use both positive instances and negative instances of a new concept; tell what it is as well as what it isn't.
5. Pay special attention to structuring the end of your lecture. Reemphasize key points; suggest job-related action based on the key points; send trainees home with a challenge.
6. Prepare a handout summarizing the key points for trainees to take back with them after the lecture as a review of training.

ADVANTAGES

1. It is economical.
2. You can handle a larger group of trainees.
3. You have good control of time and content.
4. You can easily use your lecture notes again.
5. Lectures can be videotaped for showing later.

4: Workshop

Your management team of 15 executives has gotten together to write a corporate policy statement. You begin the workshop with a single group session in which you lay out the three basic parts of the quality policy: (1) a statement about five lines long that is the policy itself; (2) a list of the responsibilities of each employee regarding policy implementation; and (3) a list of the responsibilities of each manager regarding quality development and policy implementation. You then divide the class into three groups of five people. Each group becomes a workshop whose task is to tackle one of the three basic parts of the quality policy. The goal is to create the quality policy by the end of the training session through combining the work done in each workshop.

SUGGESTED PRESENTATION TECHNIQUES FOR THE WORKSHOP

1. Give the class an overview of the quality policy—why it is important and what elements should go into it.
2. Give the class an exact idea of what you want: a policy statement of no more than five lines, a section outlining the individual employee's responsibilities regarding quality implementation, and a section on the responsibilities of the manager in developing quality. Write this structure on the flipchart or blackboard, or project it on a transparency, for all to see during their workshop session.
3. Give trainees instructions applicable to the formulation of written statements, such as the need for parallel grammatical structure, the advantage of starting every directive with an active verb, and the need to be sure each item is possible to do.
4. Break the larger group into small groups and define each workshop's task. Be sure each group is clear about what its task is and what its outcome is supposed to look like.
5. Provide each workshop with pads of paper and pencils, flipcharts and markers, and any other equipment (for example, tape recorders) that it might need.
6. Be sure each workshop has a leader. Give the leader some freedom in how to approach the task. Suggest having a recorder in addition to a leader.
7. Walk around to observe each workshop in action. Intervene only when you are obliged to answer questions or resolve conflicts.
8. Focus on your goal of getting a quality policy completed by the end of this training session. Conduct a wrap-up session of all trainees at which a spokesperson from each workshop presents workshop results. Give the group as a

whole a chance to make modifications. Ask one person (or do it yourself) to review the whole policy for consistency and accuracy of expression.

ADVANTAGES

1. Actively involves most trainees.
2. Is focused on an outcome or result.
3. Enables group members to share ideas.
4. Forces participants to support and work with each other so that the group can progress toward its goals.
5. Tends to focus on actual problems, thus serving as a motivator for trainees to learn the techniques for dealing with these problems.
6. Is usually very job-related.

In Brief

This chapter has given you some general and specific guidelines on planning training for groups of employees and has shown you techniques for doing the training yourself. Examples of group training situations have been described throughout the chapter.

The following checklist can serve to refresh your memory and guide your thinking about how to train groups of employees.

MANAGER'S CHECKLIST 4

How to Train Groups of Employees

_____ 1. Think of a class of trainees as a collection of individuals who will exhibit more differences than likenesses.

_____ 2. Give as much attention to managing the group dynamics as you do to delivering the content of the course.

_____ 3. Be organized. Practice using instructional materials and media.

_____ 4. Learn every student's first name and use it many times during training.

_____ 5. Move around; get trainees involved with you and with each other.

_____ 6. Use question-and-answer techniques deliberately, alternating between "closed" questions and "open" questions.

_____ 7. Listen to your trainees.

_____ 8. Give feedback to the class as a whole as well as to individual trainees.

_____ 9. If you use handouts and manuals, show the trainees how to use them effectively. Don't just dump them on the class.

_____ 10. Prevent problems from arising by using different techniques for facilitating group tasks and group processes.

_____ 11. When conflict occurs, manage it.

_____ 12. Allow 20 minutes per lesson, but plan on only 15 minutes of instruction. Balance each lesson with explanation, experimentation, and feedback on the trainee's progress.

CHAPTER 5

How to Train Long-Distance

Sometimes trainees are separated geographically from their instructor. This instructor might be you, or it might be someone you have chosen to represent you. In either case, the responsibility for delivering good training rests with you.

Long-distance training has been with us for a long time—through instructors who travel with their courses from branch to branch or factory to factory, and through correspondence courses. It has been given a new look in recent years by electronic options made possible by advances in telecommunications, television technology, and computers.

Long-distance training has characteristics of one-to-one training, peer training, and group training—and sometimes all three combined. Each type of long-distance training is a compromise between the most desirable face-to-face kind of training, expediency, and cost. Each type of long-distance training builds in some human contact between trainer and trainee.

This chapter presents an overview of long-distance training, including both the traditional ways and the newer ways of delivering it. Topics include suitcasing your course, training through correspondence courses, teletraining over land lines, videoconference training via satellite or local area networks, interactive video training using videodisc plus personal computer (PC), and computer-based training (CBT) via mail and telephone.

This chapter provides you with a description of each type of long-distance training and suggests the decision parameters you'll have to consider if you're faced with having to train long-distance. In each case, you will have the option of being the instructor and designing the training. In each case, you might prefer to entrust these functions to someone else. The decision parameters section of each type of long-distance training will help you to make those design and delivery decisions. The description of each type of long-distance training concludes with a list of some of its typical training applications to spark your imagination in case you'd like to try something similar.

Traditional Long-Distance Training

In spite of the electronics revolution, two older methods of long-distance training are still very much in use.

Suitcasing

Suitcasing a course simply means packing it all up in a suitcase or box, loading it into your car or an airplane, or sending it by ground carrier to a remote classroom. Suitcasing is done when classroom training is required but when travel costs for students who are geographically dispersed are too high to bring them into the central training center where you are located.

Suitcasing carries some risks with it. Often the classroom at the other end is not well equipped, well lighted, or climate controlled. It is often in a strange location, so that workers on the loading dock who receive your box of materials don't know where to deliver it. Things can get lost in transit, or you may forget to load up something essential. It takes time and coordination at the remote location to get the materials to their proper destination on time. Often there is no training support staff there to help you, or even anyone who understands or cares about training.

For these reasons, you may be tempted to skimp on the course design, to pare down your handouts and media use to what can fit into your briefcase or carry-on bag. You may try to avoid having to use a binder-type student manual because it's too heavy. Such compromises might decrease the effectiveness of your course.

Despite its risks, there are situations where suitcasing is the obvious answer. Use suitcasing when:

- The course is best taught in a group.
- Trainees are located at long distances from you.
- Trainees are located in many branches, factories, stores, and offices where their presence on the job is critical and the business can't afford to have them travel.
- Travel and lodging expenses for trainees are too costly.
- You are the best instructor for this training.
- You can make the time and have the budget to travel.
- You have better support services for getting training materials together where you are located than the remote locations have available to them.

TYPICAL TITLES OF SUITCASED COURSES

Training the Trainer	White-Collar Quality
Time Management	Performance Appraisal
Designed Experiments	Advanced Statistics
Problem-Solving Techniques	Product Realization Process

Correspondence Courses

A correspondence course is one that travels by mail to a trainee, with an instructor (or team of instructors) located at a remote office location. Generally, there is no classroom or face-to-face instruction. Trainee and trainer commonly interact by telephone on an ''as needed'' basis.

The typical trainee by correspondence does independent study and practice at home on lessons that are mailed at intervals by the correspondence school. Staff instructors at the correspondence school offices grade the trainee's assignments and within a week or two return them to the trainee with comments and suggestions for improvement.

Correspondence courses can lead to new skills if they feature practice materials designed to develop skills. Very often, these kinds of correspondence courses come with models, simulation devices, tools, and real problems to solve. Correspondence courses can lead to certification and credentialing. They are generally designed for a mass audience.

A variation of the correspondence course that is purchased from a correspondence school is the course you design yourself and mail to your employees at remote locations. It's easy to send along a videotape, samples of products, or other learning aids with your printed lesson materials to make the course interesting. You may find this an attractive option in certain situations because it still gives you some control over your trainees' learning if you run your course according to a prescribed mail-out/mail-in schedule, check the trainees' work yourself, and are available for telephone consultations.

Correspondence courses are advisable when:

- Individual trainees are located in many diverse geographical sites.
- The course as it's written is appropriate for each of these trainees.
- Training can be spread over several months.
- The course's objectives are your objectives.
- All trainees are at about the same level.
- All trainees are working toward the same goal.
- Your trainees can probably stick to the schedule imposed by the course.
- Your trainees are good independent workers and can probably tolerate the lack of face-to-face contact with the instructor.

- Your trainees are motivated by the outcome of the correspondence course—for example, certification or an advance in salary grade.
- You have sufficient interest to monitor their progress.

TYPICAL TITLES OF CORRESPONDENCE COURSES

Level 2 Certification
Principles of Financial Planning
How to Repair Wiring Boards
Office Interior Design

Russian Grammar
Real Estate Licensing
Models for Management
Essentials of Inventory Control

Electronic Options

The proliferation of electronics devices and systems in recent years has of course vastly increased the types of training available and the number of people who will receive training.

Teletraining Over Ground Lines

Teletraining is training delivered by using telephone lines to carry a training program to distant trainees and to carry their questions and responses back to the instructor who initiates the transmission. Two basic delivery modes are used: audio and audio plus graphics (audiograhic).

The instructor teaches from an office, classroom, or conference room. The presence of several trainees at the transmission location with the instructor lends an atmosphere of reality. Basic teletraining requires an audio talk-back system (audiolink) to provide two-way communication between the transmitting office or "classroom" and the remote receiving classroom(s). Any place reachable by telephone can be a receiver of teletraining, which makes it a powerful and quick means of delivering training to a widely scattered work force. Teletraining is especially appropriate for knowledge-based training; it is less appropriate for skills-based training. Audiolinks allow all the participants in the remote locations to hear each other's concerns and responses, thus increasing the likelihood of generating new ideas, solutions to problems, and interactions that might not be possible any other way. A good teletraining instructor is sensitive to all the remote learners and brings them into the interaction by effective questioning and feedback.

Because teletraining is electronically controlled, both trainer and trainees have to get used to interacting with each other through the intermediary of speakers and telephone equipment. This cuts down on spontaneity. In addition, many people feel the need to have eye contact with an instructor before they respond. Each remote receiving location requires a site coordinator/technician or remote training specialist (if you're lucky, it's the same person) to set up the receiving equipment, show trainees how to use it, coordinate and prepare your visuals or handouts, and keep the remote students focused and participating.

Audiographic transmission can include images such as letters, numbers, and lines (graphs, tables, circles). These images are generated by such devices as computers, word processing systems, electronic graphics pads, light pens, and facsimile (FAX) machines, which means that these devices have to be available during sending and receiving. Freeze-frame video technology can also be used to transmit still video images. New technologies allow full-motion video to go from both transmitting site and remote sites over high-speed, high-capacity digital lines. Most companies that use teletraining do not make extensive use of full-motion video because of its high cost.

Teletraining that includes audiographics is more expensive than audio-only teletraining. Because trainees are used to graphics and visual stimuli during training, most good teletraining offers some audiographics. The most inexpensive and often the most effective audiographic teletraining is done simply by FAXing a copy of the instructor's overhead transparencies, product description, engineering specs, memos, or other critical documents pertaining to the topic of the training to the remote sites shortly before the teletraining transmission. The remote site training coordinator makes transparencies of the FAXed documents and uses them in the remote classroom on a conventional overhead projector as the instructor teaches from the originating transmission site.

Costs of teletraining include production equipment, extra telephones and signaling devices, loops and connections, remote site technicians, receiving equipment at each remote site, large-screen projectors if graphics are used, and testing time prior to transmission. Simple teletraining can be very inexpensive if electronic conference rooms are already set up in your company and you don't require special audiographic capabilities. Tele-training can also be done using conventional speakerphones at both ends of the transmission. Teletraining services are available through nationwide long-distance carriers, local telephone companies, and businesses that specialize in these kinds of business services.

Teletraining is the appropriate choice when:

- The knowledge base in your subject is constantly changing.
- Employees all over the country need to understand this critical new business development and must learn how to use the information within a few days.
- A huge backlog of students exists for a particular course.
- One particular instructor is a treasured corporate resource, the only person who can say the right things about the subject and the obvious person to whom students should be exposed.
- The course is short (one to three days) and can easily be taught in one-hour modules spread out over several days.
- Site coordinators are available.
- Site technicians are available.
- You have a well-planned course that is suitable for teaching through the question-and-answer technique.
- You're creative enough to figure out some instructional techniques to increase the appeal of the course and make trainees see its relevance to their jobs.
- You can handle the faceless anonymity of your trainees.
- You have practiced keeping track of who is speaking from which remote site.

TYPICAL TITLES OF TELETRAINING COURSES

Engineering Fixes for the P6 Pump
Tax Law Updates for Corporate Accountants
Expected Challenges from Foreign Competitors
Improving the Weekly Readout of Quality Progress
How to Use the Chairman's Daily Pick of the Best Securities
Three Cases of Overbooking
Seminar on Robust Design
New Warnings About Drug #5252: What to Tell Physician
   Clients

Videoconference Training

Videoconference training is training delivered across hundreds of miles via satellite and over short distances via local area networks. It is video training coming from an instructor in a studio to trainees at remote sites equipped to receive the video broadcast. It is sometimes known as business television, and it generally comes with the capacity for both ends of the communication to see each other and interact with each other on one or more TV screens (video monitors).

Because transmissions run the risk of being captured by anyone who taps into the same beam, the originating transmitter must take certain precautions: either not to transmit proprietary company information or else to electronically scramble its transmission. This limitation should be considered before designing the training program.

Videoconference training is a media show, and therefore requires staging and production similar to any TV production. When you create your training materials, you must pay attention to colors and line quality; you have to learn how to speak and look directly into certain cameras (usually there are at least four: a fixed camera, a camera focused only on the instructor, a camera focused on the students, and a documents/graphics camera); you might have to learn to use a teleprompter and an electronic graphics desk; you must learn how to move in a certain way; you need to be aware of the best way of conveying information (for example, by interview, commentary, dialogue, dramatization) for the medium of television; you are obliged to adapt your teaching techniques to what the camera can convey best.

All these things cost money. Videoconference training is very expensive up front. You'll probably need professional help from a graphics production studio and possibly from a writing studio to get your materials and your lesson itself in shape. You'll also have to pay for all the equipment and hookup charges (satellite or local area network), testing time, per-hour transmission charges, and studio production services such as lighting, makeup, set design, program director services, studio rental, and field engineering services for the remote classrooms. If you're looking for these services, contact your long-distance telephone carrier or a business that specializes in satellite communications (if you need to transmit across country).

Some companies already have video transmission networks. They might have been installed for financial, legal, marketing, or public relations departments, and you may not be aware of their existence. Before you "go commercial," check around within other departments in your corporation to see if an existing network could be used for training. Videoconference training can be cheaper than you think if your company already has some of the setup you require.

Videoconference training should be employed when:

- Remote trainees need to see images of what's being taught.
- Trainees are scattered and have an immediate need to know certain information that will be internalized more easily through television.
- The large number of trainees can justify the cost.
- Employees' workplaces have receiving capabilities.
- The need to know is critical to the business.
- Very high-level people or specific innovations ought to be broadcast.
- Per-employee cost for training-related travel has gotten out of control.
- You have excellent studio services available.
- You believe the appeal of television will enhance learning.

- You have the money.
- The corporate culture supports "high tech" in its human resources functions.

TYPICAL TITLES OF VIDEOCONFERENCE TRAINING COURSES

How to Demonstrate the New Power Wand to Customers
What's New in Biscuit Dough
What FDA Approval Means for Drug Sales
Optimal Office Setup to Process Claims as Well as Clients
Learn Prospecting Techniques From the Pros
How to Set Up Custom Kitchen Services Displays in Stores
How to Survive a Chemical Fire
Update on Contract Negotiations and Strike Activity

Interactive Video Using Videodisc Plus Personal Computer

Interactive video is essentially a self-paced learning medium that allows the trainee to interact with persons and processes that are viewed on a TV screen. These persons and processes have the capability of being programmed to behave in many different ways so that the trainee can see the immediate effects of his actions. Trainees generally find this kind of learning very appealing. In order to learn this way, the trainee must have a videodisc player, a video monitor with an interactive controller such as a light pen/touch screen, and a personal computer (PC) with hard disk and floppy disk drive (or a commercially available system that integrates all these pieces of hardware).

Because of the individual nature of such learning, interactive videodisc training has a great potential for effecting savings in time, travel, and facility maintenance over the life of a course. There is, of course, no need for training staff or training center. However, because of the long development time (months or years) required to create a course on interactive videodisc, the subject matter of such courses is somewhat limited. This kind of technology has wide applications for subjects that are generic, such as sales strategies, safety procedures, and operational methods, but it is limited for subjects that have a critical time-dependent characteristic. Because of the cost of development, you want to be sure that the course will be around for a long time and not quickly become outdated. Reprogramming costs time and money, and so does making new videodiscs.

You can purchase this kind of training from large computer manufacturers with well-developed educational and training organizations. Check into buying ready-made lessons as well as into purchasing system components and the capability of creating your own training programs.

Interactive videodisc PC training is appropriate when:

- A large and diverse trainee audience is out there.
- The subject is rather generic.
- The subject is highly visual and interactive.
- Trainees will learn best through trial and error, experiencing cause and effect in a compressed way, and the challenge of repeated practice.
- Trainees are motivated to learn on their own by interaction with television.
- Your corporate technology supports this kind of training.

TYPICAL TITLES OF INTERACTIVE VIDEODISC PLUS PC COURSES

Monitoring Vital Signs

Interviewing Techniques for the New Personnel Representative

How to Terminate an Employee

Essentials of Conflict Management

Incorporating Fashion Influences of Rome, Paris, and Madrid

Conversational Chinese: Tone Production and Consonant Close-ups

Sales Power Strategies for Success

Closing Techniques for End-of-Month Operations

Computer-Based Training via Telephone and Mail

Computer-based training (CBT) via telephone has been nicknamed "Dial-Up CBT" because it is activated simply by making a telephone call to a computer that contains training software. Another version of Dial-Up CBT is CBT by mail, through which periodically you get a floppy disk containing your training program—a sort of CBT-of-the-month club. In both cases, trainees are scattered geographically, learning is self-paced, and the instructor is invisible.

This training option is attractive to companies whose employees are computer-literate and who have personal access to computers (a terminal to a mainframe in every office or a PC on every desk). CBT does not work very well if the trainee has to leave her own office and go to another room. CBT works best when the trainee can spend an hour or two at her own convenience at her own terminal or PC in between other work.

Users of Dial-Up CBT must understand the limitations imposed by the nature of the training program that is resident in only one computer. There are capacity limitations to a computer's memory and to the user's ability to get quick input and output. Dial-Up CBT is often a good choice of training delivery for managers who are accustomed to using electronic networks and who understand the way they work.

CBT has been around for several decades, and has been used successfully in training situations that are "linear," that benefit from immediate feedback to the individual learner, and that require drill and practice. Dial-up CBT or CBT by mail are distance learning alternatives to traditional CBT delivery.

Purchase this kind of training from companies that specialize in custom computer-based training development and installation. But be sure you already have the right computers or the funds to buy them.

CBT via telephone and mail training is a good option when:

- Potential trainees are very comfortable using computers.
- A modem is available to every trainee who wants to use Dial-Up CBT. (CBT has to be easy to do or trainees will not bother. They're essentially on their own as learners, and they don't need roadblocks, especially at the front end of training.)
- Excellent training programs are resident either in the main computer or on floppies. (Check them out first yourself to

be sure the CBT programs were created by good training designers as well as by good programmers. Be sure that the medium is not the message.)

- Your system administration for handling training is in place.
- You have some way of knowing who's using the training services and what their progress is, that is, when you actually can expect to have a better trained work force.
- Your main computer can tolerate the sporadic drain on capacity and input/output processing that Dial-Up causes. (Training can sometimes tie up the computer at critical business processing times. You'll need to know whether or not you require dedicated training times and memory space.)
- Your subject is enhanced by what computers do best— calculations, rapid branching, variety and speed of feedback, organizing and reorganizing information, presenting options.

TYPICAL TITLES OF CBT VIA TELEPHONE AND MAIL COURSES

How to Back Up, Move, and Copy Files
Designing Arches
Effects of Lowered Interest Rates
Balanced Portfolios
Diagnosing Neuropsychological Problems
Optimal Fixes for Engine Knock
Relationships of Policy Changes and Employee Disability
Market Parameters for Test Markets and Sampling

Reference List for Electronic Training

The following brief, focused reference list is included to help you pursue current industry and professional information in various electronic training fields. The training associations listed in Chapter 7 will also be helpful through their special interest groups in video and electronic training.

Associations

Association for Educational Communications and Technology
(AECT)
1126 Sixteenth St. NW
Washington, D.C. 20036

Boston Computer Society
One Center Plaza
Boston, Mass. 02108

International Interactive Communication Society (IICS)
2120 Steiner St.
San Francisco, Calif. 94115

International Television Association (ITVA)
6311 N. O'Connor Rd., Suite 110
Irving, Tex. 75039

Society for Applied Learning Technologies (SALT)
50 Culpepper St.
Warrenton, Va. 22816

Periodicals

AV Video
Montage Publishing
25550 Hawthorne Blvd.
Torrence, Calif. 90505

Business Television
Telespan
P.O. Box 6250
Altadena, Calif. 91001

BYTE
70 Main St.
Peterborough, N.H. 03458

CBT Directions
Weingarten Publications
38 Chauncy St.
Boston, Mass. 02111

CD-I News
Link
79 Fifth Ave.
New York, N.Y. 10003

Data Training
Weingarten Publications
38 Chauncy St.
Boston, Mass. 02111

Teleconference
Applied Business Telecommunications
Box 5106
San Ramon, Calif. 94583

Videodisc Monitor
P.O. Box 266
Falls Church, Va. 22046

Video Manager
Montage Publishing
25550 Hawthorne Blvd.
Torrence, Calif. 90505

Books

Advanced Interactive Video Design by N. V. Iuppa and K. Anderson. Knowledge Industry Publications, Inc., White Plains, N.Y. (1988).

Disconnection: How To Interface Computers and Video by G. A. Souter. Knowledge Industry Publications, Inc., White Plains, N.Y. (1988).

Educational Technology Publications. 720 Palisade Ave., Englewood Cliffs, N.J. 07632. (Send for catalog.)

Interactive Toolkit by D. Gayeski. Knowledge Industry Publications, Inc., White Plains, N.Y. (1988).

A Practical Guide to Interactive Video Design by N. V. Iuppa. Knowledge Industry Publications, Inc., White Plains, N.Y. (1984).

Secrets of Video Training: Training With Video Casebook by S. R. Cartwright. Knowledge Industry Publications, Inc., White Plains, N.Y. (1989).

Teletraining Means Business by L. A. Parker. Center for Interactive Programs, University of Wisconsin Extension, 610
Langdon St., Madison, Wis. 53715 (1984).

Training With Video by S. R. Cartwright. Knowledge Industry
Publications, Inc., White Plains, N.Y. (1986).

In Brief

This chapter has given you an overview of long-distance training—training in which the instructor or source of instruction is
separated from the trainee. It has been developed to show you
the evolution of long-distance training, to help you isolate the
decision factors concerning long-distance training, and to spark
your imagination as to the possibilities of using this training
option when you can't train face-to-face.

The following checklist allows you to review the options
available for conducting your long-distance training.

MANAGER'S CHECKLIST 5

How to Train Long Distance

_____   1. Suitcase a course if your trainees can't leave
their work locations and they need to have classroom instruction.

_____   2. Choose correspondence courses if you can
spread learning over a period of months and can
stick to the mail-out/mail-in schedule. Consider
writing and administering your own correspondence courses.

_____   3. Consider teletraining for knowledge-based,
word-intensive training that must reach a wide
audience quickly.

_____   4. Consider videoconference training if you want the power of television to enhance your objectives—and you have plenty of money.

_____   5. Choose interactive videodisc training for generic kinds of visual subjects that employees can learn independently.

_____   6. Verify the quality of instructional design of any CBT course. Dial up a CBT lesson if machine space is available. Be sure any CBT is user-friendly and accessible.

CHAPTER 6

How to Get the Most Out of Your Company's Training Department

Face it. Sometimes you need help. When the role of trainer is more than you care to perform yourself, when you have too many employees to be trained, or when you need a customized course with trainee and instructor manuals, you need to call in the pros. If your company has a training department, that's the first place to look.

This chapter helps you work with your company's training department to get the biggest bang for your training buck. It shows you how to ask the piercing questions; suggests where you can give a little and where you must stand firm; and helps you to get the most for your money from the pros, keep your bottom line intact, and get the best services for your employees.

Investing in Training

The first thing you ought to remember is that buying training, even from your own in-house resource, is a business deal. You are putting up the money and getting a service, perhaps some products in the form of training materials and manuals, and are expecting a good return on your investment. If you approach the training manager as a customer, chances are that you'll get what you need from the training department. Just make sure you are treated like a customer with very special training needs and with very specific requirements for training.

The Customized Course

If your company employs instructional designers, you can probably reap the benefits of having them write a course just for you. On the other hand, human resources specialists who function as coordinators of outside seminars or as registrars and schedulers cannot design a customized course.

Be sure to "ask around" about the competencies and qualifications of the persons in the training department before you request a customized course design. Go this route only if you have training pros who have expertise in curriculum design, in the choice and use of instructional materials, in adult learning theory, and in evaluation design. Be wary of a training specialist who offers to pull together something from this course and something from that course to make up your course; this hodgepodge obviously would not be a well-planned course, truly customized to meet your unique requirements. A customized course should begin with planning for your needs and with a discussion about learning.

Figuring the Hidden Costs

Be prepared to spend money on good training. Keep in mind that the price of having untrained, unproductive employees is heavier still. A commitment to training pays off in better performance, increased productivity, and greater profits. These benefits of training don't come cheap. You can expect to get your money's worth, but you can also expect to have to pay a fair price for training developed and delivered just for you.

Analysis

Take a look at what typically goes into training. The training pros talk about a systems approach to training that starts with the process of figuring out what you really want. This is called "needs assessment," "needs analysis," or sometimes just "research." They'll engage you in conversation about learning "objectives" and your goals for the course. If you don't pay for this analysis process directly, you pay for it indirectly as part of the up-front costs of training design.

Allow the trainers to go through this with you, but put a time limit on the endeavor so that you don't get analyzed to death. Stay involved with the trainers as they interview employees or look through your documentation; monitor the time they spend on the task. When analysis paralysis sets in, it's your responsibility as manager to move the process along.

A good, focused needs analysis is a great idea, but what you really want is for the training designers to get on with the design of the training itself. Your best guarantee of value in the needs analysis process is to support the pros and to monitor them. A good approach to the trainer is to say, "Needs Assessment? Wonderful. I'll be available to provide you with whatever documents you need, and I'd like the results in ten days."

Design

Following the needs analysis, the training department will tackle the job of writing your course and producing your training manuals. During the design and development of training, all sorts of hidden costs generally surface. Be prepared to fund your part of a graphic artist's time, an instructional technologist's time, writers' and editors' time, typists' and production workers' time. Be prepared to pay for the paper and other supplies used during the various drafts of your course. Be prepared to pay for an evaluation design. This might include exercises for the trainee during the course as well as a customized course evaluation form to be completed by each trainee at the end of the course.

When you get hit with a seemingly larger dollar figure for a course from the training department, consider this guideline: it takes about 50 person-days or two months to write a customized one-day course. Add to this the time it takes for you to review the draft of the course and for the training department to make revisions. Ask the training manager to give you an honest estimate of all the variables of cost that go into the final cost. Be aware of what's happening during course development, and be willing to pay for a thorough job. Well-designed training is worth its weight in gold.

Delivery

Delivery of your training is a process full of hidden costs too. First, the instructor will need a day or two of preparation with the course manual and materials in hand. Additional time might also be required for a dry run of the course, especially if it involves use of specialized equipment, computer hookups, lab sessions, or if it is the first presentation of unique conceptual material or new technical material. As the customer, you want to be sure that the course as you approved it on paper can, in fact, be taught.

It pays off in the long run to take the extra time to deliver the course in front of a small group of "fake" students. Insist on enough time to do this, and enough time for the instructor and course writer to get together afterward to make revisions before the course is given to your employees. You want the best possible course, designed and delivered to be well-balanced, devoid of extraneous information, and structured so that people can learn. Training pros know how to get a course together, and they function well in this "try it out and revise" mode. You'll definitely come out ahead if you fund this predelivery effort. You might even want to be involved in choosing the "fake" students.

The instructor's travel expenses are also part of the costs of delivery. If you have a large group of employees or several large groups to be trained, pay for the instructor to come to you. Trainers sometimes call this "suitcasing" a course—that is, the instructor and the course travel to you. It's a lot cheaper to pay one person's travel expenses than to pay for all of your employees to go to the instructor. Figure also that there will be some costs associated with the transport or mailing of course manuals, handout materials, and supplies that the instructor uses in teaching.

It's far better and more cost-effective to incur these expenses and to have your own employees remain on the job as long as possible. Time spent away from the job in attending class is expensive enough. Don't also spend precious time and money on employee travel and lodging.

The Training Department's Off-the-Shelf Course

Often the training department will have a course in its library of courses that is precisely what you need for your employees, just as it is. This kind of course is known as an ''off-the-shelf'' course because it can simply be pulled off the library shelf and presented to the trainee audience in pretty much the same way it has always been presented.

This kind of course is often tied to specific equipment or products or to specialized business processes generic to your company. Examples of such courses are ''How to Load Programs Into the Computers in Our Computer Center,'' or ''Key Characteristics and Demonstration Techniques of Our New 5253 Copier,'' or ''An Explanation of Our Benefits Package Including Recent Contract Items Regarding Retirement Benefits.''

As off-the-shelf courses or seminars are standard for most audiences, costs of development and delivery are minimal. When you buy this kind of course from your training department, focus on the efficiency aspects of it, since the content is already designed and apparently acceptable. That little extra value added often shows up in the way the many coordination factors work together to make the course run smoothly. Because they've done it before, the scheduling, registration, course evaluation, and feedback to you will probably be done correctly and in a timely fashion. Truly professional training departments have enough staff to handle the details efficiently—and you'll benefit accordingly.

Off-the-shelf courses can be a great boon to you because they are not too expensive and generally have good track records for delivering training that works.

Delivering the Course to Your Employees

The costs of course delivery are both obvious and not so obvious. The obvious ones are the instructor's salary, the trainee manuals and materials, the consumable flipcharts, markers and note pads, audiovisual materials, food and drink during breaks, and rental of the classroom. As the customer, you should have assurances that these items are taken care of and that they are of good quality. Make it a point to inspect the manuals and trainee materials and to view slides or transparencies at random to be sure that all projected words are readable and that handouts and manuals are clear and visually attractive. The quality of training is often prejudged by the feel of the manual in a trainee's hand. As a customer, you need to know that it feels right—before your employees make that judgment.

The not-so-obvious costs of delivering instruction are found in the behind-the-scenes operations of scheduling, registration, and coordination of evaluation forms. The training department has people who are pros at doing all these things, each of which can be a big headache for an ordinary manager. It's well worth it to have the trainers perform these operations because they're the ones set up to do them right.

Accounting and Accountability

What you can expect from the training pros regarding these not-so-obvious costs is a careful accounting of who signed up on time, which employees are slated to go to class at what time, what the agenda of each day of class will be, who actually showed up for each session of the course, a summary and analysis of the evaluation forms completed by students, and a timely bill at the end of the course.

Trainers will talk to you about whether or not your goals for the course were met and about whether or not your employees accomplished the objectives for learning that you established. When you get the evaluation summary and analysis, pay attention to the statements regarding the learning objectives. Don't pay your bill until you're satisfied that your employees learned what you intended them to learn.

A well-crafted and skillfully implemented "training system" for your course should contain the elements of analysis, design and development, delivery, and evaluation. You should be able to observe members of the training department carrying out these processes over the period of time they are working for you. Shortcuts will inevitably result in less learning, less value for time expended away from the job, and less ultimate impact on the corporate bottom line.

When you engage trainers to work for you, expect them to develop your course within this systems framework. Accountability from them should include your involvement in the system's inputs, outputs, and feedback.

Check out the training department ahead of time. Sit in on a course similar to the one you are having written; or, better yet, take a course that interests you from the people who will be designing or teaching the course you have in mind.

The Bang for Your Buck

Just what is it that happens during training? What are the secrets that ensure good training? What kind of training leads to the most learning, the best attitudes, the greatest improvement in skills, and the fastest payoffs? What do you look for in a course or an instructor to put your mind at ease that you're on the right track to getting the most bang for your buck?

Improving Performance

When the training pros design and deliver training, they write and teach so as to enable their trainees to improve their performance. This kind of instruction is seldom done in a lecture format, and seldom carries any assigned homework. Trainers are careful to specify—with your help and sign-off—certain objectives for that particular group of trainees. Each of these objectives carries with it a standard of performance, such as "... with 80 percent accuracy," "... to achieve a perfect bond," "... in nine out of ten tries," "within five minutes." It's the instruction tied to specific objectives that pays off in terms of performance improvement.

You can spot good training because it has been carefully crafted to motivate trainees toward accomplishing specific job-related objectives and to guide them through discussions and exercises built around those objectives. If you want a good idea of what might happen during the training of your employees, ask the instructor to let you see all the objectives for the course. Check the standards to be sure they are high enough yet achievable, and check the content to be sure it leads toward achieving improved performance.

Some managers prefer that the training designers prepare a list of all the objectives of the course before they write up any lessons or develop any training exercises. Even if you're using a tried and true off-the-shelf course with a good record of effectiveness, it's still a good idea to read through that course's objectives just to make sure that they are what you think they are. The employees for whom you are responsible and your corporate bottom line both deserve the best possible course you can provide.

Involving Trainees

The first clue to good training is the activity level of the class sessions. In general, the more active the classroom, the better the chance for good training to occur. Look for sets of small groups working on problems; look for trainees handling flip-charts or presenting reports; look for a roving instructor. Look for animated discussion. Look for laughter.

Remember that adult learners at work are primarily workers, not students. They work to make a living and to make a contribution to their job. Most people want to do a good job, and want to improve themselves and the financial picture of their company. Adult learners in training have a job focus and an action bent.

They will not be passive learners, and will generally rebel at passive instruction. Be sure no one lectures at them! Be sure that the training is structured for the maximum involvement of trainees in labs, job-related exercises, and give-and-take discussions, and that this will be accompanied by plenty of feedback to individuals and plenty of reinforcement and encouragement. Training pros will know this, but it doesn't hurt for you as the customer to leaf through the instructor manual to be sure that lots of action is built into the course and into the instructional methods.

Another clue to good training lies in the application opportunities that are written into the course. Adult learners want to use their new skills and knowledge right away to improve their jobs. Adult learners like to wrestle with real or very closely simulated problems. They want the chance to learn and practice new skills quickly; they don't have time for much theory.

The aware customer will make sure that the course is long on application and short on theory. The wise customer will also make sure that enough flexibility is built into the course—the kind of flexibility that allows digression in order to address problems the trainees might bring to class. Trainee-initiated problems or questions often get to the point of the lesson more quickly than the instructor's prepared materials do.

Balancing Between the Big Three Types of Training

Trainers like to talk about three major types of training: training to help people acquire new knowledge (cognitive training), training to help people acquire different attitudes (affective training), and training to help people acquire new skills (psychomotor training). Courses can be made up of all three types of training, of only one type of training, or of some combination of two types of training. If you do one-to-one training or group training yourself, these are the same three types of training you will be concerned with in those situations.

As a customer of your training department, you should have

a clear idea of two things: (1) the balance among the three types of training that is available for your course, and (2) the level of instruction that is or will be designed into each type of training—for example, beginning skills training, advanced attitudes training, intermediate knowledge training. Training often misses the mark because it has been designed at the wrong level for the class or with an imbalance regarding the type of training. As a customer, you have a responsibility to describe your training needs regarding balance and level to your course designers as carefully and accurately as possible.

If you choose to use an off-the-shelf course, you have an even greater responsibility to verify the appropriateness of the level of instruction. What might seem like a cost savings in using an off-the-shelf course instead of a customized one could turn out to be a costly error if the prepackaged course is pitched either too high or too low for your particular group of employees.

Knowledge

Getting the most bang for the buck out of knowledge training means that the instruction is so designed that the trainee can return to the job and easily integrate that new knowledge into his work. It means that the content of the course doesn't stay closed up in the manual on the shelf!

The wise manager can spot elementary knowledge training if the course manual contains too many lessons that simply require the trainee to recall, list, identify, or restate. More advanced cognitive tasks are to formulate, analyze, revise, solve, evaluate, synthesize, and verify. Don't accept a customized course that is too elementary. Talk with the pros first about the level of cognitive tasks they feel is right for your course.

In order for training to stick, it has to be designed at the correct level for the trainee to translate it into improvements on the job. It does no good to write a course full of identification exercises when what you really want is for the trainee to be able to troubleshoot a problem and formulate an approach to solving the problem. Cognitive training has to match the cognitive level of the objectives you've set.

Almost all training has some element of knowledge training in it. The training pros should have the experience to design into your course the appropriate techniques for your diverse class-room of trainees to acquire all the knowledge they'll need. Check with the pros on this by simply asking them about the "level" issue, and weigh their answers carefully to be sure you think they're right.

Attitudes

Getting the most bang for the buck out of attitude training means that an attitude change will quickly be felt in the trainee's work environment. This can be measured by such means as attendance reports, productivity measures, frequency counts, and usage logs.

Attitude change can be directed at the trainee herself, as in training to help angry or frustrated workers. Or, training for attitude change can be directed at people like salespersons or supervisors who are responsible for changing attitudes in others. Sales training often has a strong affective training thrust directed at changing the customer's attitude. Supervisory training often includes attitudes toward leadership and skills for dealing with attitudes toward and attitudes of subordinates.

The trick in this kind of training is to correctly identify the ways in which to measure its success. If you engage in this kind of training, it's incumbent upon you to check with colleagues in the personnel department or with your legal advisors to be sure that the questions you want to ask your trainees are fair and nondiscriminatory and that the focus of your attitude training fits in with corporate personnel policies and practices. Also be sure that the success of your attitude training can be measured.

Skills

Getting the biggest bang for the buck in skills training means that the trainee can go directly from class back to work with new or improved skills that are securely enough learned and practiced to use on the job. Skills training requires demonstra-tion and practice, feedback, and corrective action during class.

If you purchase this kind of training, be sure that lab sessions, skill exercises, practice, and time for trial, error, feedback, and correction are designed into the course. One of the worst mistakes in training design is to design a skills-based course that allows too little time for truly learning new skills. As a customer, be sure that your course has only enough knowledge-based training to enhance and clarify the skills-based training. A skills-based course that is loaded with "identify" and "define" exercises probably won't teach your employees new skills. Rather, look for words such as "build," "modify," "move," "set," "lift," "place," "open," "depress," "view," "align." Psychomotor training involves eye-hand coordination and the use of muscles. Well-designed skills training includes training in preparing for the correct action, training in responding to cues, and practice so that consistent performance is possible.

Asking the Right Questions

As a non-trainer, you are somewhat at a disadvantage when it comes to communicating your training wishes to the training department because you are not as familiar with training jargon as they are. Here are some questions to ask that speak in the trainers' language and that will set them on the right track toward designing and delivering a good course for you:

1. May I help you establish the learning objectives for the course? When?
2. May I check the scope and sequence of the course content when you have the first draft ready? When?
3. Will you be sure to design exercises and assessments that are specifically tied to an objective of the course? May I verify this while the course is still in draft form?
4. May I see the course evaluation form you intend to use at the conclusion of the course so that I can be sure it is focused on getting the kinds of information I want?
5. What will the materials of the course look like? Is there a trainee manual? Are there slides or transparencies? Are there handouts? What is your review process for guaranteeing legibility, good graphic design, and clarity of ex-

pression? May I or someone I designate be involved in this review process? When will the materials be ready?

6. What are the choices of delivery methods for this instruction? Which do you prefer? Why are these better?

7. How will I know that my employees actually made it to class, and how will I know that they learned anything?

8. What's the best way I can help you to help me?

9. How long will it take you to design the course and run a field test of it? How much time do we need for revisions?

10. (If the course has been given before): May I read the evaluation forms from the last few groups of trainees who took this course? What steps have you taken to correct any problems identified on these evaluations?

11. How many sessions of the course do we need?

12. When shall I block out the time that I need for review and for the training itself? What does your development schedule look like?

13. How can I let my employees know what the current opportunities for training are?

Standing Firm

As the customer of the training department, you have a right to receive value for the course you purchase. These are the items on which you should stand firm:

• *Verification of the need for the course.* Be sure that the course is needed and that the improvement you seek cannot be achieved by any other means (for example, policy change, bonus, meeting, monitoring and documentation, punishment). Training pros are trained to help you verify need. Use them for this purpose.

• *Review and sign-off on learning objectives.* Do this as soon as possible.

• *Review and sign-off on course content.* Do this as each unit of instruction is completed if you have the time. Or, if time is short, review and sign off on groups of units that are similar or that depend upon one another.

• *Field test of the final draft of the course in front of real people*. Insist that your trainers allow time in the development schedule for this.

• *Evidence that the instructional designer and the instructor have considered alternative ways of delivering your course*. Before the trainers begin writing a course for you, be sure that they can tell you why certain ways of presenting your training are better than others. Some options are more costly than others, and you should be given the alternatives with an honest appraisal of the chosen method's appropriateness and value.

• *A customized course evaluation form for trainees to fill out at the conclusion of the course*. Because they're your employees who are taking the course, you want a systematic way—in writing—of determining what they thought of the training. The smiles test as they exit the classroom is not enough. You also want to know how that kind of training could be improved the next time it is given to similar employees.

• *Accurate record-keeping during the course*. As the person who's paying the bills, you have a right to know who was there for each session of the course, who was late, who was cooperative, who caused trouble. You also deserve a timely bill with as much backup accountability data as you desire.

• *Feedback to you from the instructor after the course*. Your deal should include formal and informal feedback from the instructor regarding your trainees' accomplishments and regarding the design of the course.

Bending

Sometimes, in order to keep the peace or to strengthen your negotiating power, you need to bend a little. In dealing with the training department to get your course together, these are the areas regarding which you can afford to bend:

• *Complexity and duration of the needs assessment*. A needs analysis does not have to be very lengthy, and its complexity may vary. All you need is assurance that what you believe to be a training need is in fact a training need. Let the trainers figure out how to do this, expending as few resources as possible.

• *Type of field test.* You can bend on the type of field test. That is, you can abbreviate the field test. You could omit some of the lecture-type descriptive or explanatory material. You could omit showing all the slides. You could choose representative examples of exercises or lab experiments. You could choose to field test only those lessons which you believe will be particularly troublesome. You could use draft copies of manuals and handouts. A field test does not have to be of the entire course, word for word.

• *Choice of delivery method.* You might have to compromise on the choice of delivery method if your budget is too squeezed by what you thought would be nice. For example, use of a prepackaged videotape to convey information might be cheaper than engaging the training department to write half a day of a course to do the same thing.

You might have to give up your perception that a lecture course by a big-name trainer in the corporate training center would be the most cost-effective training. Maybe just as good training would occur if your employees could view the videotape at their convenience during the regular work day on the borrowed VCR in the conference room adjacent to your office. Let the trainers come up with the best choices, and bend a little if you have to.

• *Lapse time for feedback after the course is finished.* Don't make the instructor stay late to talk with you immediately after the course. Teaching is exhausting, and especially if the instructor has a plane to catch and leftover materials to pack up, you can afford to wait a few days for your feedback. If the class ends a little early, catch the instructor then. In either case, show up to thank the instructor and to indicate that you'll be expecting feedback and course evaluation results within two weeks.

• *Comprehensiveness of the trainee manual.* Good teaching will compensate for poor written materials. If you are pressed for development time, consider using a minimal trainee manual, more easily reproduced handouts, and wall charts to present information. However, realize that trainees like to take something home with them as a means of refreshing their memories about what they have learned in class. Compromise on the trainee manual issue only if you know that your instructor is top-notch.

The Bottom Line

The bottom line is that you want employees who are more productive, more highly skilled, and contributing maximally to the department's and the company's profits. You have chosen training as the best way to achieve these things. Performance, productivity, and profit are what it's all about. Well-designed training will get you there, and the test of success is in the measurements that will change to show you just how your employees are stacking up in these three important facets of work.

Your job as manager is to think carefully about the most direct routes to the bottom line. By all means choose training, but be sure that your standards are in order, that your analysis of work tasks and the workplace is complete, and that your measures are fair and consistent. Training is a worthy corporate player with great promise for contributing to corporate financial health. Call in the training pros—and give them some well-informed guidance—to help create the kinds of courses that are just too much for you to handle yourself.

In Brief

This chapter has highlighted key issues in dealing with your company's training pros and has provided suggestions for getting the best in-house training for your training dollar. You've seen where to look for hidden costs, what to look for while a course is being written for you, and how to communicate what you really want to your training pros.

The following checklist summarizes what you, as a manager, can do to get the most out of your company's training department. It will help keep you on target as you balance your responsibilities as a manager of employees with training needs and as a guardian of your company's financial health.

MANAGER'S CHECKLIST 6

How to Get the Most Out of Your Company's Training Department

_____	1. Remember that buying training is a business deal.
_____	2. Look for a systematic development process in customized courses.
_____	3. Put a time limit on needs assessment.
_____	4. Participate in the design reviews of customized courses.
_____	5. Insist on some kind of field test.
_____	6. Bring the instructor to you.
_____	7. Let the trainers do all the administration.
_____	8. Sign off on objectives for the learner.
_____	9. Be sure the course is action-oriented.
_____	10. Be sure the course is long on application, short on theory.
_____	11. Look for a balance of knowledge, attitudes, skills.
_____	12. Look for the appropriate level of instruction.
_____	13. Check the trainee evaluation form.
_____	14. Ask for feedback directly from the instructor.
_____	15. Check the course materials for clarity and legibility.
_____	16. Verify standards of productivity.
_____	17. Verify criteria of performance.
_____	18. Choose training for the right reasons.
_____	19. Be reasonable about the time it takes to develop a course.
_____	20. Support your trainers as they support you.

CHAPTER 7

What to Do If You Can't Do It Alone

Training sometimes works best in collaboration with outsiders. Before you commit your time and effort, think about whether you can pull together some external resources to do the job better.

This chapter helps you to decide if you need outside help and provides guidelines and suggestions on how to find it—and how to use it to your advantage. In it you learn what's involved in a training proposal, how to deal with consultants and contractors, what to expect from equipment manufacturers, and how you can make use of colleges, universities, and local adult education programs. There are also tips for controlling quality among the unknowns of using outsiders, and some addresses of professional associations that might help. A special section on workplace literacy offers guidance on ways to approach this increasingly critical training need.

Decision Factors

Successful training is a business operation that is subject to all the constraints governing any other business operation: whether it can be done efficiently, effectively, and with positive impact on the people involved; whether it ties in directly with corporate goals, and can be effected in a style consistent with the corporate culture; and whether it is relevant in terms of what the competition is doing and what the corporate financial position is.

As you begin to think about involving outsiders in your training operation, focus on the following six decision factors, listed here in priority order:

1. *Customers.* How can this training best affect my customers? Should customers be involved as planners, instructors, or students in this training?

2. *Economics.* How will this training affect my budget? What impact will it have on my department's cash flow and stated expenses for the year? If I hire a full-time trainer for this project, how can the company make use of this person when the training is finished? Is it better to "build" or "buy" this training? Will a consultant fee be cheaper in the long run than funding employee benefits and salaries? Can I borrow or barter any part of this training?

3. *Technology.* Do I need outside expertise because of advances in technology? Do I have the right hardware, software, equipment, or scientific know-how within the company? Can I find more knowledgeable technologists outside? Might it be less expensive to rent the technology I need for the duration of the training in order to provide trainees with the latest and greatest? How important are "bells and whistles" as corporate image-builders and as motivators for trainees?

4. *Information.* Can someone outside my sphere of influence do a better job of presenting new information to my trainees? Might someone else be better versed on new policies, new procedures, new product information, new legislation, new marketing strategies, or new competitors? Can bringing in someone else save me learning time or provide my trainees with greater breadth of knowledge or important new contacts?

5. *Objectivity.* Are the circumstances within my organization/ corporation such that an objective point of view would be helpful? Might an outsider serve as a catalyst for change or be

useful in causing opinion to gel or in facilitating communication? Can an objective voice working with us speed our training program along?

6. *Public relations.* Do we have good reason for increasing our community visibility or our reputation as a good corporate citizen? Might it make sense to engage community leaders in our training project as advisers or instructors? Are we looking for a rate increase from a public utility board? Do we have an impressive affirmative action program that we'd like the public to know about? Have we made an impact on basic literacy? Are we faced with important environmental problems and solutions? Do our safety practices warrant publicity? Are we creating many new jobs for people in our geographic area? Have we stemmed alcohol and drug abuse among our workers? Is our fitness program worth talking about? Will election results affect our business?

How you answer these questions will guide you in your decision regarding collaboration with outsiders. Talking over some of the issues raised by these questions with colleagues in your corporate human resources, marketing, and public relations departments will help you zero in on the best outsiders to contact. Remember that the bottom line is the bottom line—that your goal as a manager is to give your people the best training possible for the dollar you have to spend.

The Training Proposal

If you decide to go outside for help, you'll probably have to convince your boss that the services or products you seek are worth the money. To do this, you'll probably be asked to write a proposal describing and defending your decision.

There is a range of acceptable proposal styles within the fairly standard constraints of the boss's need for clarity of expression, accurate cost figures, and a plausible rationale regarding value. All proposals should include:

- A statement of the objectives of the proposed training
- Information about the employees who will benefit from the training
- A description of how you will interface with the proposed service or product from outside
- An accurate description of what you intend to purchase
- The entire costs of implementing the proposal
- A statement of the terms and conditions you agree to regarding payment for the proposed training service or product

In addition to including the standard information in any proposal to management, you should master a few tricks of the proposal writing game if you want your proposal to be taken seriously.

Making It Short and Sweet

Very few bosses enjoy reading long detailed documents. Keeping this in mind, try to make your training proposal short and sweet. Short means two or three pages; sweet means positive, true, and somewhat sales-oriented.

If you feel compelled to give your boss a lot of backup documentation showing how great your proposed solution is, do this by appendices or another folder of "Related Information." Also, don't be tempted to spell out in great detail exactly what you intend to do when . . . ; save the detailed implementation schedule for the later operational phase of your project, or put the schedule in an appendix. The proposal itself is best if it's short. Remember, the purpose of the proposal is to get funding.

Selling to the Top

A nice trick in proposal writing is to use the statement of objectives in a sentence or two to open the proposal. You do not have to state your objectives in a cold, impersonal outline or bulleted list. It's even better if you can start out the proposal by clearly relating the objectives to a corporate goal or to some "hot button" that you know will cause your boss to react.

Some examples might be, "In an effort to continually improve customer information systems. . . ." "Because this corporation has a public commitment to providing a safe work environment. . . ." "It is a stated goal of this company to pass decision making and budget responsibility down to first-level management. Therefore, . . ." When your very specific objective(s) follow such a statement, it then seems quite rational and very much in the corporate interest to consider funding what you request.

A brief, accurate statement of what you want to purchase follows the opening statement. This section can be called something like "Essential Elements of This Proposal" or "Description of the Proposed Course" or "Key Characteristics of the Proposed Service." Remember that your boss is a busy person who probably doesn't care about the complete table of contents, operating instructions, and twenty testimonials regarding your proposed course, product, or training service. It's important, of course, for you to know this information and to have it ready in case it should be called for, but including it as part of the proposal can bog down the reader and tempt him to put the proposal aside to answer a phone call or to turn to a more interesting problem of the day.

Writing to the top means structuring your writing so that all the accountability information is presented simply and clearly. This accountability information typically includes: what its payoff is, what it is, when it will happen, and how much it costs. It's so much easier to make a decision about committing resources when the parameters of the decision are succinctly laid out.

Getting the Yes First

At the end of reading your first two sentences regarding the proposal's objectives and their relationship to a corporate goal, your boss should be able to say, "Yes, of course I agree with this." Or if you've had to strike a somewhat dissonant chord in your opening statement, you'd want your boss to be able to say, "You know, she's right" or "You bet! He's certainly on target."

The point is that you want to create the atmosphere of "yes" right at the top of your proposal, even as early as just after the first sentence or two. If you are proposing to address a particularly sticky issue, you might even want to expand upon your statement of objectives in a second paragraph that ties your rationale and proposed solutions to the probable target audience and expected benefits in terms of this target audience. Again, however, choose your words carefully, don't pad your prose, and keep it short and sweet.

Go for a series of yes reactions to the statements you make on the first page of the proposal. When you get to the costs on the second page, your chances of getting that ultimate yes will be that much greater.

Consultants and Contractors

Consultants and contractors are hired for temporary periods to work on specific projects. Typically they are paid by the day or by the hour, and work within your organization for about six months.

There are various levels and types of consultant services and independent contract work. Contractors are generally persons who work for themselves and are independent of any umbrella consulting firm. Contractors are often technical experts such as computer programmers, software designers, evaluation specialists, scientists, or artists with highly focused and specific skills.

Contractors are generally paid per hour and paid directly. Consultants, by contrast, are often members of a consulting group or firm who are paid a salary by that firm based on charges to you at a per hour or per diem rate. Obviously, with such consultants, the firm takes a markup to cover its overhead and make a profit.

What Do They Offer?

Consultants offer a variety of services ranging from high-level strategic planning and organizational diagnosis to computer system documentation and writing training manuals. Consulting groups offer experienced advisers who work for a high per hour fee or young workers who function as helping hands and work for smaller per hour or per diem fees. Consulting groups can provide you with a single worker, a pair of workers, or a whole team of workers, depending on your needs. Some consultants also sell "influence" such as political contacts or high-level negotiations within a specific industry. This chapter does not include a discussion of influence peddlars.

STANDARD TRAINING SERVICES OFFERED BY CONSULTANTS

- Advising high-level decision makers (you, your boss, your boss's boss)
- Facilitating task forces and committees
- Contributing technical or specialized input to course designers on your staff
- Developing a plan (for example, a training marketing plan, an affirmative action plan, a safety awareness plan)
- Evaluating or assessing an existing program
- Creating a course from a review of current documents or new technical developments (for example, reviewing marketing plans and studies to create a new course on market strategies, or reviewing current successful applications of a new statistic to create a new generic R&D course)
- Designing a curriculum (for example, six courses for account representatives, three required courses and three optional courses for secretaries, four required supervisory skills courses)
- Writing a course manual (for example, user guides, instructor manuals, trainee manuals)
- Teaching a course
- Presenting a packaged workshop (for instance, on Time Management, Interviewing Techniques, Effective Presentations)
- Designing a test
- Designing an evaluation system and evaluation documents
- Coordinating a conference
- Providing research (for example, on white-collar crime in

this industry and its implications for management training, or on the uses and abuses of computer-based training for new account representatives)
- Preparing instructional videos
- Preparing instructional slides and transparencies
- Designing and producing instructional charts and job aids
- Brokering services such as printing, packaging, and mailing

Finding the Good Ones

Finding good consultants is not always easy, although plenty of them are out there looking for business. You should choose one with the same care you'd use to choose your personal physician. Does the consultant have a good reputation in the specialty in which you need help? Has the consultant been in business long enough to have both breadth and depth in training design and delivery? Will the consultant's personality help the project? Do you inherently trust the consultant to make good decisions and to be honest? Do you believe that the consultant will deliver value and quality? Think about these questions as you prepare to contact potential consultants.

More specifically, you might want to investigate more fully some of the areas suggested by those questions. The following guidelines are explained in depth to help you.

Reputation

Don't just read the consultant's list of clients. Ask the consultant for a list of the project titles actually delivered to that list of clients and the dates on which the projects were delivered. You want to be sure that this consultant or consultant firm actually works in the area in which you seek help. You can't really tell from the name of the firm or its list of clients exactly what the firm does.

A reputable consultant will tell you exactly what he did and when and will give you a reference name to contact. A less than reputable consultant will be vague and use the client list to attempt to impress you. A less than reputable consultant will tell you that he can certainly handle your job; beware of this reply and be sure that you have the opportunity to make that decision yourself based on evidence in your area of special need.

For example, a computer systems consulting group might have a fine reputation in the management information systems area but no reputation at all in designing management training. Don't let the term "management consulting" fool you—ask enough questions to be sure of your potential consultant's reputation in the area of your need.

Business Breadth, Depth, and Longevity

If you choose to deal with a consulting firm, be sure that you respect the business practices of that firm. Some consulting firms hire only part-time consultants who work on specific projects and are then terminated. Other firms hire full-time employees who are experienced in the specialty of the firm and can handle a range of assignments with a variety of clients. Generally, the firm with full-time employees has been in business for some time, has a strong core of loyal and experienced consultant employees, and can offer you breadth and depth of analysis and implementation skills. Firms with full-time employees can also generally offer you replacement consultants of similar quality in case a consultant assigned to your project becomes ill or leaves the firm.

If you aren't sure about the business strength of your potential consulting group, try to find out from associates who have used them previously just how long they've been working in the area. Find out by phoning the business office of the consulting firm how long they've been in business and what percentage of the consulting staff are full-time employees. Find out what percentage of the firm's business is repeat business or referral business. Both these percentages should be 80 percent or more to indicate breadth and depth in a particular consulting field.

Check the business office for some indication of the stability of the staff. A high turnover rate among professional or support staff could indicate a poorly run firm. Check, too, to see that the firm has adequate support staff—word processors, high-speed printers, secretaries, clerks, graphics specialists, editors, accountants—to accommodate the number of professional staff. If the proportion of support staff to professional staff seems too small, you may have good cause to fear that the "back-office work" of production could delay your project.

Find out who the principals of the firm are and how long they have been associated with the firm. Look for a firm that has been in business for at least ten years, with principals having at least five years' service.

Find out if the firm employs salespersons or account reps in addition to consultants. Most consultants want to "do the work" but object to having to sell it. The firm in which consultants must also be salespersons could be a sign of weakness.

Take steps to assure yourself that you will be comfortable with the remuneration practices of the firm you select. For example, some firms pay their consultant employees a rather low per hour wage but encourage them to work overtime at the client site. This may boost the take home pay of the consultant, but it's not clear that your paying the extra hours of overtime wages will provide you with more than a day's necessary work. Ask a principal of the firm how the consultants are rated and measured. Does the answer assure you that the consultant's ability at project management is a strong part of the measurement criteria? If you get the message that bringing in more dollars is the primary criterion, make an exit. Greedy firms don't attract the most able designers and deliverers. Consultants who are successful at their work have generally been around for awhile and are happy enough with the pay.

Hiring an independent contractor (who may be called a consultant) carries with it less risk regarding reputation and business practices. This is because the contractor works alone or with minimal help, generally has very little overhead, generally is the sole recipient of the fee you pay him, and is secure in reputation because he is an experienced specialist. Although the issues surrounding reputation and business practices are more self-evident with contractors, the basic questions posed at the beginning of this section apply equally to both contractors and consultants.

Personality and Personal Characteristics

Most seasoned consultants will tell you that good consulting is about 90 percent good "chemistry." The occasion for calling in a consultant is when you need help, and generally need it fast. You don't have the time or inclination to work with someone new to make him fit into the organization. You want a consultant who is pretty much like your current staff in personality, who will fit into your corporate culture easily, and who can "hit the ground running." Look for someone like yourself or like your organization in temperament. Look for someone who seems flexible and easy to get along with. Much of consulting's success depends upon the facilitation and acceptance of small changes within your organization. A consultant with personal characteristics that match those of your organization can work more effectively with you.

Trust

Finding a consultant you can trust to make good decisions is a matter of checking credentials and giving the potential consultant a chance to demonstrate integrity and genuine interest in working with your business. Do your paperwork before you interview a potential consultant. Be sure the person's work history and academic records are in keeping with what you expect him to do for you.

Plan an extended interview—at least an hour to be sure that the potential consultant really has a good feel for your business and believes he can make a significant contribution to it. Be sure that the person's credentials are not "top heavy" for your organization. That is, structure the interview in such a way that you have assurance that the potential consultant can start at the level where you are and will not be too academic or become frustrated by a mismatch in understanding.

Don't be afraid to share with the potential consultant some of your tough problems so that you have a chance to see whether that person responds appropriately and with integrity and consistency. You are not looking for a "yes man" who will say anything to get in the door. In your interview, try to get the potential consultant to express his views of the big picture of your problem and to identify several of its smaller components. A person you can trust is a person you will feel has your best interests in mind.

Above all, you want to believe that value and quality will be delivered by the consultant to whom you entrust your problems, your staff, and your money. Belief is largely a subjective thing, hard to quantify and hard to defend. After you've done as much checking into reputation, business practices, personality, and trust factors as you possibly can, the decision to choose a consultant boils down to your belief that this person can set into motion the processes and deliver the products that will solve your problem in the best way. Finding good consultants is both a science and an art.

Using Them Right

Using consultants right is largely a matter of knowing what you want, defining the role(s) you want the consultant to perform, and having a plan for the engagement.

Knowing What You Want

At times of stress or organizational upheaval, when you are likely to need an outsider's help, it is often hard to think perceptively and clearly. Before you call in a consultant, do the best job you possibly can of specifying what you want. For example, do you want advice? a new product? a major change in direction? only a hint of change? Think about the end of the consultant's stay with you and visualize what it is that you want him to do at the project close-out meeting. Do you visualize a slide presentation full of flow charts and prioritized lists or do you visualize a 400-page binder containing a new course on Quality Management? Be as specific as you can be in determining what you want to result from the engagement before you make the first contact. Knowing what you want will help the consultant price your job correctly and will spare you the necessity of later having to refocus the project.

Defining the Consultant's Role

You'll get the best service from a consultant if you can clearly define the role or roles you want that person to perform. Consulting is a support service, not a mainstream operation of your business. Always define the consultant's role within this framework, keeping the mainstream business operations for yourself. In other words, do not allow the consultant to take over—and do not force him to do so. Most consultants are in the consulting business because they like to get in and get out of projects; they like the variety of working in many different situations and for many different businesses. They generally are not very good at taking over—they want to support you and let you handle the decision making.

There are many support roles a consultant can perform, among them, to do research, to provide information, to advise, to structure, to change, to teach, to evaluate, to design, or to produce a product. Your task as a manager is to be sure that the consultant understands which role you want him to perform. Of course, it's okay for you to want a consultant to perform several roles—for example, to do research, to evaluate, and to advise; or, to write and to teach. Just be sure that you and your consultant are both very clear about when one role stops and the other role starts. You will get better value and better cost estimation from a consultant with clear role definition, and the people in your organization will be able to interact more successfully with the consultant whose role is well defined.

Having a Plan

Both the consultant and your accounting department will be happiest operating under a plan for the consulting project. The basic elements of this plan are management, monitoring, documentation, and communication.

• *Management.* First, be sure everyone knows who's boss. Assume the job of project manager yourself or appoint someone else to be in charge of the consultant's time with you. Be sure that a single person is ultimately responsible, and that the consultant knows who this person is. Don't force the consultant into a "wheel and deal" mode of operation because of uncertainty about who the real client is. Project quality will suffer if you allow this to happen.

Your accountants will also be happy to know that there's just one audit trail connected with a specific project, with one person authorizing payment. Because consulting money is often coming from "somewhere else," that is, not from the regular budget, you need to be especially sure that the financials of the project are well handled.

• *Monitoring.* This goes along with management responsibility. As with management, monitoring ought to be the responsibility of a single individual, although others might be involved in small-scale data collection or monitoring activities during one of the many processes that go on during a consulting engagement.

Monitoring should be clear and structured. Both the consultant and your staff need to know how you define the standards of consulting performance, when and how you will judge the quality of the consultant's work, and how you will provide feedback to your staff and to the consultant.

In setting standards, be reasonable. Remember that consultants are helpers. They're human beings at work, subject to the same troubles that plague all persons at work—they get sick, they miss deadlines, they misplace things, they get caught in traffic. Sit down with your consultant to get his ideas regarding a monitoring plan and schedule. Don't use monitoring to play "I gotcha" with anyone—your staff or the consultant. Be fair, be clear, be organized, be professional.

• *Documentation.* Writing things down is generally time worth spent when you're dealing with consultants. Good documentation makes you as the client feel more secure that work is being done, and it makes the consultant feel that his efforts are producing some results.

Be sure that the consultant knows what format you prefer (for example, outlines or narrative reports) and knows exactly when you expect documentation to be provided (for example, every Monday, every two weeks on Fridays, or with the final bill for services). After you receive the first piece of documentation from the consultant, give him some feedback regarding its acceptability. Realize that documentation takes time, and that you are ultimately paying for it. Structure your documentation requirements carefully so that you get only the documentation you need; otherwise, you'll end up paying for more paper than service.

Consider alternatives to paper such as videotape or audiotape, both of which make excellent documentation media. If you have a consultant whose home computer can communicate with your computer, consider electronic mail on a periodic basis to satisfy your documentation requirements and to save time.

• *Communication.* Communication is critical during consulting engagements because of their typically short duration in the operational life of a company. In dealing with a consultant, you simply don't have the time to correct misperceptions and fallout from communication mistakes. Simplify matters for yourself by choosing a consultant with whom you are comfortable right away, one who communicates the same way you do. If you tend to be a little loose and action-oriented, don't hire a consultant who seems uptight and overly wordy. Keep looking till you find one who fits in better with the way you operate regarding information.

Talk with your consultant often. Don't allow him to go off and do the work alone or to disappear into a cubicle with a computer. In the end, you'll feel that you've gotten more of what you expected to get if you've regularly spoken with your consultant about how things are going, what his findings are, and what kinds of "vibrations" he is getting from being with your staff. Consultants are tuned in to listening for what's happening in an organization. Make it a point both to give and to seek feedback. You'll save time and money and possibly generate new ideas and better solutions if you invest in good communication practices.

Equipment Manufacturers

Training problems that you can't solve by yourself often occur in connection with the purchase or lease of a major new piece of equipment. Examples of this kind of equipment are computers, accounting machines, word processing equipment, printing or graphics equipment, testing equipment, design equipment, photographic equipment, copy machines, fire detection systems, sound amplification systems, and simulators and mockups (themselves used for training) such as flight simulators, power generation simulators, refinery process simulators, refrigeration system mockups, and electrical system mockups.

Often groups of people or key individuals must know how to operate this equipment, but there's no one to teach them how to do it. In acquiring a major new piece of equipment the focus is usually on installing it with the least disruption to existing systems and spaces and on getting the thing running. People seldom get excited over learning how to use it properly and thoroughly until well after the account rep has gone on to another account.

Knowing What to Ask For

The wise manager will anticipate the moment of truth when the equipment breaks down for the first time and the salesperson is long gone. The wise manager will ask the account rep at the beginning of negotiations for some assurance that training will be provided as part of the deal, and that it will be conducted in concert with the installation schedule for the equipment.

The equipment manufacturer can reasonably be expected to provide at least some of these kinds of training and training support: how-to manuals, user guides, on-line user courses, troubleshooting and failure detection guides, a panic button service or telephone hot-line customer support service, a hands-on class or seminar either at the supplier's site or on your site after the equipment is ready, video demonstrations of the machine's capabilities and close-up techniques for getting the most out of the machine, and possibly a site representative who functions as a one-to-one trainer when the new equipment is put into service.

Being Realistic

Training is generally not a major reason why the equipment manufacturer or supplier is in business. Chances are that the equipment manufacturer does not have on staff instructional designers or persons who know how to write training manuals. What seems obvious to the engineer, industrial designer, or craftsperson, however, is not that obvious to the person on your staff who needs to learn how to use the equipment.

User guides are notorious for being imprecise, unclear, and not particularly user-friendly when they are written by technical builders who are not specially prepared to help people learn their way into the operation of a new machine. If you get user guides with your equipment purchase, check them out to be sure they are adequate. If they are not, make plans either with your account rep or without him to hire an experienced trainer to work with your staff to teach them how to use the equipment.

Your account rep may know someone who is experienced in teaching the skills for using the particular equipment you are purchasing, and, at the very least, can put you in contact with that person. However, be prepared to have to make these arrangements yourself and probably to fund them yourself too.

Being realistic about the services you can expect from an equipment manufacturer includes being realistic about the amount of time that a manufacturer will be willing to give you once the equipment is up and running. If you suspect that your staff will have a lot of trouble with this new machine, try to pin down your account rep to agree to a specific time period for troubleshooting and on-the-job training facilitation. Realize, however, that learning theory and human relations skills are probably not top priorities with the personnel who may be assigned to troubleshoot or assist you with training. Respect the manufacturer for technical expertise, and be willing to bend a little in the human resources development area. Be prepared to assign your own OJT facilitator to your staff.

Videos demonstrating how to make the equipment work can be very valuable aids to learning. To be most effective, the video should be used at or near the equipment, should be accessible to all who might need it, should feature closeup photography demonstrating exactly how to do a particular process, should be technically correct and complete, and should be free of any sales pitch.

Colleges and Universities

Colleges and universities are a convenient and willing source of help for many kinds of training. Those that have business or management programs are especially good bets, and those with departments or programs of study in the area in which you need help (for example, Chemical Engineering, English as a Second Language, Video Communication, Statistics) are also likely places to contact. Community or county colleges, private colleges, and universities with graduate schools are all good places to look for knowledgeable individuals and courses that just might be ready-made to help you out.

Think for a moment about how colleges work and about who goes to college these days. Most students go to college to prepare for a career. Programs are organized around the skills and information a person will need to work in a particular career field. People of all ages and experience levels go to college, as the pace of change in the workplace creates the need for more and more people with new skills and the know-how to do another job. If you look through a college catalog, chances are that you will find a course or a contact person that is just what you need. College instructors these days are used to having adults in class, and they are becoming increasingly able to relate to the needs of adult students with a career focus. They may be very familiar with students who are much like your employees. It's also easier these days for students to take a course or two without being pressured into signing up for a four-year degree or a long-term commitment.

A word of caution, however, is in order. Some professors teach courses from a very theoretical and academic perspective, even though the course may sound practical in the catalog description. If you want to send your employees to college, talk with the professor first to be sure that the course as taught is practical enough for your purposes.

Choose a professor with some business experience. Ask the professor to include some examples from your company if possible. Provide him with case studies or data from your business so that the course can be tailored to your employees' needs.

If possible, get the professor to come to your training center or conference room (even the employee lunchroom can be turned into a training room) to deliver the course. This will save your employees travel expenses, parking hassles, and time. Arrange for some kind of college credit to be given if that is important to your employees. Work out a simplified registration procedure. Remember that employees at work generally don't want to be students, so make student life at work as free of obstacles and as work-related as possible.

Institutions of higher learning offer a wide variety of educational opportunities to choose from. Four of the most obvious places to investigate for people and programs that will help you to meet your training needs are suggested below.

Continuing Education

Most universities and many colleges have a Continuing Education Division that is designed to reach out to the business community with practical courses in a wide variety of career fields. These courses are often given in the form of a seminar rather than as a semester of classes. Some of the more common topics offered are accounting and finance, secretarial and support services, general management, marketing and sales, personnel administration, health and safety at work, data processing, and computer applications. Many continuing education seminars are marketed through direct mail flyers sent to persons whose names are on selected business mailing lists.

Most instructors in continuing education seminars are persons who have been employed in business for a substantial period of time, or consultants who work in a variety of businesses in addition to teaching a seminar several times per year. The typical seminar lasts three to five days and is held at a hotel. The university coordinates the program, recruits the instructors, and operates within a set of guidelines that assure the participant of the program's educational value.

Continuing Education Units (CEUs) are often granted to participants at the completion of the seminar. The CEU is a nationally recognized indicator of continuing professional achievement. One CEU is granted for every ten contact hours of instruction. Some companies encourage employees to accumulate CEUs as an indication that they are keeping abreast of current business developments.

Continuing education seminars can often be tailored to your employees by making special arrangements with the university and the instructor to bring the seminar to you. Look into this if you have a group of employees who need rather generic training (for example, in basic word processing skills, basic spreadsheet applications, basic statistics, time management techniques, basic project management tools, or what's new in desktop publishing). A university or college continuing education operation can be flexible and is in business to help people just like you.

Institutes and Centers

Colleges and universities often have institutes and centers associated with them. State bond issues, legislation, or foundations created by individuals and businesses are generally the source of funding of such organizations. These institutes and centers often have a research and development charter, and may be tied to a specific industry. Examples are the Center for Laser Research, Institute of Public Policy, Center for Labor Studies, International Marketing Institute, Center for Plastics Research, Biotechnology Institute, and Center for Architectural Innovation.

You could be in luck if the training you need happens to be in the area of specialty of a nearby institute or center. You could expect to get from such a center or institute the latest information about the specific field, but you might not get the best teaching if the center is primarily a research operation. It's worth inquiring about training through such a place if your training need is technology-based and very specific to the work of the center.

Such centers might be able to offer you training of a nonconventional kind by allowing your employee to spend one-to-one time with a university researcher for a specified period or by allowing him to sit in on research team discussions.

Funding constraints might prevent such flexibility, but it's always worth inquiring if you believe the match is just right. You might even be able to work out a barter deal whereby you get the training you want in exchange for allowing a graduate student to do an internship project on site at your company.

Professors and Grants

Professors at most universities and at some colleges are responsible for getting grants from major funding sources so that they can pursue research in their fields of specialty (for example, medical cost containment, financial planning, quality management, competency test design, market planning, computer networks). Many grants to academicians are made with the provision that the business community have some input in the proposed project so that there is a better chance of the project's findings leading to practical advances. If you get to a professor before the proposal writing is started, you might be able to write yourself into the grant in some way and do the professor a favor at the same time.

The major problem with academic proposals is that they generally take a long time to get funded and even longer to be implemented. Three years is a fairly standard period of time from the professor's idea to the first results from the special program designed under the grant. Your training need may be too immediate to permit waiting so long. But if it isn't an immediate need, and could benefit greatly from some kind of collaboration under a specific grant, by all means contact the professor who functions as the department head in the subject of your interest and take it from there. Find out if any grants are in progress and if anyone is willing to talk with you.

Courses for Credit

The most obvious educational opportunity offered by a college or university is the course for credit. If you expect to have your employees take a number of the courses offered by the university, you might want them to matriculate into a specific program of studies that can eventually lead to a degree. Many employees will prefer being on a degree track to simply taking courses. Other employees will not want to make a commitment to a degree program or to the term papers, final exams, and theses that might be required.

If you embark upon a degree program option for your employees, realize that many employees are already overextended in terms of the time they have available; they have families, play tennis or basketball, go to church choir practice, do community work, or care for elderly parents at home. It's sometimes a hardship for people to go back to campus for an evening and to do all the homework associated with a course after putting in a full day of work. Figure out some incentive for those employees to keep going—offer a tuition refund if good grades are maintained; offer time off to go to the library; offer salary increases or bonus points after a certain number of degree credits. Be reasonable in what you ask of your employees. Remember, they are your employees because they want to work for you, not necessarily because they want to study for you.

Adult Schools

An adult school is most often administered by a public school board, which receives federal or state funds to offer educational opportunities to residents within its geographic jurisdiction. Adult schools can be found in high school districts, in regional districts, in vocational/technical school districts, and in school districts that have elementary and high schools. Adult schools are identified with a specific community or regional group of communities.

Adult schools recruit instructors who are proficient in their fields and who have a specialty that appeals to residents of the community. Adult schools have great flexibility in what they can offer, where courses can be taught, and who can be a student. Many adult schools specialize in recreational courses such as aerobics, photography, racquetball, or refinishing furniture.

Most adult schools offer some career development and business skills courses such as learning to use specific computer software, accounting for small businesses, how to write a strategic plan, technical writing, better business English, or basic business math. Fees are usually very reasonable, and group rates can generally be arranged. Adult school classes typically meet in the evening, although in many school districts with large high schools adults from the community are welcome to sit in on an existing class with the teenagers under the auspices of the adult school program. This arrangement might be helpful to you in subjects such as basic typing or conversational Spanish, or if you have a particularly young employee or group of employees who might need such a course.

Because adult schools are generally a bargain, and are conveniently located within the community, they often provide an acceptable source of skill training for certain employees. If you have identified an employee with a specific training need, check out the adult school in the community in which that employee resides. You may be pleasantly surprised at the range of opportunities available.

Meeting Local Needs

In addition to the adult school's focus on the delivery of courses is its focus on the development of courses. Often in a certain geographic area, the local business community will express a need for very specific types of training. Examples of such local needs are courses in English usage for foreign-born workers (in an area with a recent influx of Asians), résumé preparation and executive job search skills (in an area in which a major corporation has just gone through a major reduction in staff), private pilot ground school training (in an area where a busy small airport is located).

Adult schools will work with you to develop a very specific

course to help you deal with your very specific training problem. Because they are identified with a local business community, local people, and funding earmarked for the improvement of local education, adult schools are often a very efficient and extremely cost-effective source of training.

Workplace Literacy Training

As American businesses enter the competitive 1990s, they may find that their biggest challenge lies right on their doorstep in the form of a pool of available workers that has increasingly significant problems with basic literacy. What this means is that not only schools but businesses too will have to become involved in designing and delivering programs to improve the skills of workers in the areas of reading, speaking, writing, and thinking. Most companies are not prepared to offer literacy training on their own, and will seek help from outside specialists.

The numbers are alarming. The U.S. Department of Labor estimates that one of every eight workers in the country is illiterate, and that some 23 million adults across the United States lack even fourth-grade literacy skills. At the higher end of the labor pool profile are statistics showing that the state of New Jersey, for example, has one million adults who lack a high school diploma, and that 30 percent of the applicants for clerical positions at a major nationwide insurance company scored below a ninth-grade reading comprehension level in pre-employment testing. These are not isolated examples—they represent the reality faced by many states and companies throughout the country.

If you couple this with demographic projections of where the work force to the year 2000 will come from, it's apparent that many of these adults of limited literacy will be at work. Recent studies published in the *Wall Street Journal* (February 10, 1989) project that immigrants, women, and minorities will account for 85 percent of the growth in the American work force and that there will be a dramatic decline in the number of white males available and working. The historical homogeneity of American companies is disappearing.

With these changes comes the need for managers to recognize that this growing diversity in the labor pool means that bright and capable people from other countries and from disadvantaged impoverished backgrounds in this country will require training in basic literacy skills before they are able to contribute their best to business. Looked at from this perspective, literacy can be seen as a new kind of economic exchange medium that allows businesses with higher levels of literate workers to fare better in the give and take of the marketplace. Workplace literacy training can be an important strategic business tool.

Designing the Content

As you plan literacy training, think first in terms of your various target groups. Think of the specialized content each group (or individual) will need, and think of the support systems and programs your existing workers must provide for these target individuals if these people are to make the transition to higher-skilled jobs.

For Whom?

These are some of the typical target individuals and groups of employees who might need training:

- Entry-level workers for whom English is a second language
- Management-level workers for whom English is a second language
- American high school dropouts
- Persons disadvantaged because of poverty
- Older workers returning to work after years of retirement
- Workers forced into new jobs (for example, service jobs, computer jobs) because of structural changes in the nature of work

What Kind of Training?

The following content areas suggest the subject matter of literacy training:

Reading

- Rules
- Procedures
- Bulletins
- Newsletters
- Contracts
- Instructions
- Directions
- Insurance and medical forms
- Safety information
- Schedules
- Blueprints
- Software
- Specifications
- Codes
- Sentences
- Paragraphs

Speaking

- Pronunciation
- Vocabulary
- Agreement of subject and verb
- Sentence structure
- Singulars and plurals
- Social conversation
- Presentations

Writing

- Spelling
- Sentence structure
- Writing procedures
- Writing business letters
- Writing memos
- Writing to sell
- Writing to inform
- Writing to describe
- Writing to ask for help

Thinking

- Reading and writing to analyze
- Deciding what to document and in what form to do it
- Reading and writing to compare and contrast
- Reading and writing as tools to get beyond memorizing
- Expressing your opinion or evaluation in writing
- Basic business formats and systems

Delivering the Programs

Be careful about your biases when you design and deliver literacy programs and courses. As with all the other kinds of training discussed earlier in this book, literacy training has as its target audience responsible, experienced adults who want to get something from work and to give something in return.

Be sure you consider the special needs for confidentiality, safety, and advancement opportunity that this particular trainee audience has. Be creative in your choice of delivery mode. Be aware that sometimes the best approach will be an individualized one or a tutorial session; at other times, the best approach to delivery will be a group whose members can give each other feedback and support during training. Anticipate that some bright stars will come forth during your training, and be ready to suggest career development or leadership experiences for them. Consider developing a mentoring program, a buddy system, or your own in-house apprentice program for those who are outstanding trainees.

Be conscious of the probable need of your existing staff members for some "sensitizing" workshops to help them to see the value of literacy training and to enlist their help. Anticipate that they will have stereotypes about the target audience, and allow enough time for brainstorming and discussion of all issues they bring to the table.

Where to Get Help

There is good help available from a variety of sources. Programs dealing with workplace literacy can be found in chambers of commerce, local public libraries, adult schools in local high schools, community colleges, colleges and universities (continuing education programs), other companies, and consulting firms and individual consultants. The Business Council for Effective Literacy (BCEL), 1221 Avenue of the Americas, 35th floor, New York, N.Y. 10020, is an excellent source of information on current issues and programs.

Managing Quality Within Diversity

One of the biggest problems when you turn to someone outside your company for help with your training problem is maintaining quality in the service or product that you buy from the outsider. It's hard enough to maintain quality within your own organization—going outside makes it even harder. In attempting to manage quality in these circumstances, there are two essential things to focus on: setting standards for the training provided and monitoring the work as it progresses.

Setting Standards

An important part of setting standards is knowing where you want to be at the end of training, that is, having a vision of the future. It's critical to communicate this expectation to your chosen outside training provider so that everyone concerned with the project's success knows what the target is. Don't automatically assume that the outsider will give you what you want. Be sure that he knows exactly what you expect and where you expect your employees to be in terms of new knowledge and skills at the end of training.

Competency

It's a very useful exercise to list the competencies you want your employees to work on during training. If you can also determine what level of competency you are aiming for, that's even better. A list might begin by looking something like this:

1. Be able to describe all ten features of the operating system.
2. Move in and out of at least three of the operating system programs, identifying each move correctly.
3. Choose a subroutine to explore using the programmer reference manual to locate information.
4. Demonstrate thorough applications knowledge of all system message capabilities: daily bulletins, corporate and financial news, and electronic mail.

If you don't take the time to do this, you may be unpleasantly surprised when your employees come back incompletely trained or trained to do something you don't think is really worthwhile.

Trainers might call these "objectives" or "behavioral objectives." You should think of them as the competencies you want your employees to have as a result of training. Quality performance on the job will result only from people who have been trained to perform work competently. Quality seldom results from a good book, an inspiring lecture, a pleasant meeting, or a friendly instructor. A "smiles test" alone will not assure quality. Training for competent performance is the key.

Product Quality

If your work with an outsider is going to result in a training product of some sort—for instance, a manual, set of visuals, job aid, brochure, newsletter, user guide, or videotape—be sure that you tell your outsider what you require in terms of format and design. Be sure that you transmit any corporate policies and technical writing standards that could help the outsider meet your quality requirements.

Consider these kinds of standards: the company's affirmative action policies and guidelines regarding bias in written documents; type style preferences; proper ways of displaying the corporate logo and company name; copyright protection assurance; favorite colors of the department; guidelines regarding size of type for projection purposes; preferred outline style for manuals and charts; and preferred binding and packaging formats. The look and feel of a training product contributes to its quality.

Process Quality

There are two kinds of process quality to manage during an engagement with an outsider. One is the kind of project management process most often associated with timeliness and communication. The other is the development process most often associated with assurance of originality in research and relevance in design efforts.

The first kind of process quality, the management kind, is fairly easy to establish standards for and to control. Simply make it a point to sit down with your outsider and agree upon a schedule and a systematized way of communicating during implementation. That's important—don't wait until the end of a project to ask what happened. Process quality needs to be built in small stages all along the way.

The second kind of process quality, the developmental sort, is harder to set standards for and harder to control. Basically, you want some assurance that an outside seminar provider, for example, is not simply repackaging someone else's program and selling it to you as original. Just ask for a "proprietary information" statement from your outsider, or simply write a clause about originality into the contract you develop with the outsider. You don't want to run the risk of widely reproducing some nifty piece of training documentation that you thought was yours alone only to find that its source was someone you have never heard of. Copyright attorneys are in business to look at just this sort of thing. During the design phase of your training, make it a point to meet with the outsider frequently to be sure the design work you are paying for is, in fact, going on.

The other key issue in development work is the issue of validity. Is the test that's being written for you, for example, a true test of the skills or knowledge that it's supposed to be testing, or is it only one person's opinion of what it should be? Is this approach to market planning a workable and relevant idea, or is it really "off the wall" and absurd in the context of your corporate culture and implementation capabilities?

Assuring quality in design and development can often be done by involving respected colleagues in the review of design documents. You might suggest or even insist that your outside training developer name several experts who would be willing to come to a design review meeting or provide written feedback after reviewing parts of the product during the various design phases. Your best assurance of quality development is to have several design review meetings in the draft stage. Your presence at one or more of these meetings can help the designer to stay focused on your specific needs, but remember that he is the expert in the field and should probably be the leader of the meeting. You know what you want: he knows how to get it for you. You stay focused on goals, and let him worry about how to achieve those goals.

Monitoring Work

One thing all the current quality gurus agree on is that quality must be built in during the development and implementation of work. In simplest terms, building quality in means frequent, periodic, systematic monitoring of all the processes and products that are being generated while a job is being done. When you hire someone outside your company's culture, control systems, and motivation and reward devices, you may be tempted to be satisfied with defining what you want the final outcome to look like and then turning the person loose to get it done.

It's a far better idea to go one step further in the name of quality and set up a project monitoring plan before the project gets underway. The elements of a project monitoring plan might include stating the standards, defining the measurement tools (that is, frequency counts, regression analyses, pages per day, errors per line, dollars per week), scheduling the observations, communicating the results, showing evidence of integration, and rewarding high performance. Whatever the elements of your project monitoring might be, spell them out in agreement with your outsider and assign dates and reporting relationships to each element.

Professional Associations and Journals

Many professional associations are either primarily devoted to training or partially devoted to training through "special interest groups" or subassociations within the larger association. These associations are generally staffed by paid employees who are very familiar with the activities of the various chapters of the association and who are excellent sources of information about training opportunities around the country offered under the umbrella of the association. Check your local telephone directory for the phone listing of a local chapter, or contact the headquarters organization for a local referral.

The members of professional associations include consultants from large and medium-size firms, independent consultants or contractors, college professors, training product or seminar producers, and training management and support staff from large, mid-size, and small corporations. Members of local chapters of associations tend to have strong informal networks of information and relationships, and are generally happy to recommend colleagues who might be able to help you out. These associations are good sources of people who are active in their fields. Officers of local chapters can often put you in touch with a reputable consultant or corporate person who can help you to solve your training problem.

The listing below includes associations with a primary or secondary interest in training. National headquarters addresses are provided.

PROFESSIONAL ASSOCIATIONS

American Association for Adult and Continuing Education (AAACE)
1201 Sixteenth St. NW, Suite 230
Washington, D.C. 20036

American Association for Higher Education (AAHE)
1 Dupont Circle NW, Suite 600
Washington, D.C. 29936

American Educational Research Association (AERA)
1230 Seventeenth St. NW
Washington, D.C. 20036

American Management Association (AMA)
135 W. 50th St.
New York, N.Y. 10020

American Psychological Association (APA)
1200 Seventeenth St. NW
Washington, D.C. 20036

American Society for Healthcare, Education and Training (ASHET)
840 N. Lake Shore Dr.
Chicago, Ill. 60611

American Society for Hospital Personnel Administration (ASHPA)
840 N. Lake Shore Dr.
Chicago, Ill. 60611

American Society for Personnel Administration (ASPA)
606 N. Washington St.
Alexandria, Va. 22314

American Society for Quality Control (ASQC)
310 W. Wisconsin Ave.
Milwaukee, Wis. 53203

American Society for Training and Development (ASTD)
1630 Duke St. P.O. Box 1443
Alexandria, Va. 22313

Association for Continuing Higher Education (ACHE)
College of Graduate and Continuing Studies
University of Evansville
1800 Lincoln Ave.
Evansville, Ind. 47722

Association for the Development of Computer-Based Instructional Systems (ADCIS)
409 Miller Hall
Western Washington University
Bellingham, Wash. 98225

Association for Educational Communications and Technology
(AECT)
1126 Sixteenth St. NW
Washington, D.C. 20036

Association for Sales Training (AST)
P.O. Box 2748
Redondo Beach, Calif. 90278

Association of Information Systems Professionals (AISP)
1015 N. York Rd.
Willow Grove, Pa. 19090

Association of Visual Communicators (AVC)
900 Palm Ave. #BS
Pasadena, Calif. 91030

Council of Hotel and Restaurant Trainers (CHART)
Pizza Hut, Inc.
9111 E. Douglas
Wichita, Kans. 67201

Council on the Continuing Education Unit (CCEU)
1101 Connecticut Ave. NW, Suite 700
Washington, D.C. 20036

Data Processing Management Association (DPMA)
505 Busse Highway
Park Ridge, Ill. 60068

Hotel Sales and Marketing Association International (HSMA)
1400 K St., Suite 810
Washington, D.C. 20005

Human Resource Planning Society (HRPS)
P.O. Box 2553
Grand Central Station
New York, N.Y. 10163

Instructional Systems Association (ISA)
10963 Deborah Dr.
Potomac, Md. 20854

International Federation of Training and Development
(IFTDO)
923 State St.
St. Joseph, Mich. 49085

International Teleconferencing Association (ITCA)
1299 Woodside Dr.
McLean, Va. 22102

Meeting Planners International (MPI)
1950 Stemmons Freeway
Dallas, Tex. 75207

National Association of State Training and Development Di-
rectors (NASTADD)
Governmental Service Center
Kentucky State University
275 E. Main St.
Frankfort, Ky. 40601

National Commission for Health Certifying Agencies
(NCHCA)
1101 Connecticut Ave. NW, Suite 700
Washington, D.C. 20036

National Computer Graphic Association (NCGA)
2722 Merrilee Dr., Suite 200
Fairfax, Va. 22031

National Retail Merchants Association (NRMA)
100 W. 31st St.
New York, N.Y. 10001

National Safety Council (NSC)
444 N. Michigan Ave.
Chicago, Ill. 60611

National Society for Performance and Instruction (NSPI)
1126 Sixteenth St. NW, Suite 102
Washington, D.C. 20036

National Society of Sales Training Executives (NSSTE)
1040 Woodcock Rd., Suite 201
Orlando, Fla. 32803

National Speakers Association (NSA)
4747 N. Seventh St., Suite 310
Phoenix, Ariz. 85014

Organization Development Institute (O.D. Institute)
11234 Walnut Ridge Rd.
Chesterland, Ohio 44026

Society for the Advancement of Management (SAM)
2231 Victory Pkwy.
Cincinnati, Ohio 45206

Society for Applied Learning Technology (SALT)
50 Culpepper St.
Warrenton, Va. 22186

Society for Intercultural Education, Training, and Research
   (SIETAR)
1505 Twenty-Second St. NW
Washington, D.C. 20037

Society for Technical Communication (STC)
815 Fifteenth St. NW, Suite 400
Washington, D.C. 20005

Society of Insurance Trainers and Educators (SITE)
100 Van Ness Ave.
San Francisco, Calif. 94102

Training Media Distributors Association (TMDA)
198 Thomas Johnson Dr., Suite 206
Frederick, Md. 21701

Professional journals specializing in training, management, communications, and psychology are a good source of current ideas in their fields and of information about the businesses and universities where these good ideas are being implemented. Journals often have the addresses of contributors so that you can contact an author with whom you might want to talk.

These are some of the many journals in which you might find help for your training problem:

PROFESSIONAL JOURNALS

British Journal of Educational Technology
3 Devonshire St.
London WIN 2BA
England

CBT Directions
38 Chauncy St.
Boston, Mass. 02111

Data Training
38 Chauncy St.
Boston, Mass. 02111

The Educational Researcher
1230 Seventeenth St. NW
Washington, D.C. 20036

Educational Technology
720 Palisade Ave.
Englewood Cliffs, N.J. 07632

Harvard Business Review
Soldiers Field Rd.
Boston, Mass. 02163

Human Communication Research
2111 W. Hillcrest Dr.
Newbury Park, Calif. 91320

Journal of Applied Behavioral Science
P.O. Box 1678
Greenwich, Conn. 06836

Performance and Instruction NSPI
1126 Sixteenth St. NW, Suite 102
Washington, D.C. 20036

Performance Improvement Quarterly NSPI
1126 Sixteenth St. NW, Suite 102
Washington, D.C. 20036

Trainer's Workshop
American Management Association
AMACOM Publishing Division
P.O. Box 1026
Saranac Lake, N.Y. 12983

Training and Development Journal ASTD
1630 Duke St.
1443 Alexandria, Va. 22314

*Training—The Magazine of Human
    Resources Development Training*
50 S. Ninth
Minneapolis, Minn. 55402

In Brief

There are a variety of steps you can take and some precautions you should observe when you make the decision to go outside your company for help in training your employees. This chapter has given you specific sources of help.

The following checklist is a brief summary of the preceding information and can serve as a memory jogger regarding what to do if you can't do it alone.

MANAGER'S CHECKLIST 7

What to Do If You Can't Do It Alone

_____ 1. Define exactly why you think people outside your organization should do the training job for you. Can they provide better technology? Will it be cheaper in the long run? more objective? more customer- or community-focused?

_____ 2. Write a short and sweet funding proposal for your boss.

_____ 3. Look carefully for a good consultant or contractor who will match your personal style.

_____ 4. Make a checklist of questions to ask potential consultants regarding their reputation, business longevity, and reliability.

_____ 5. Have a plan for implementing any project (product or service) with an outsider. Include management, monitoring, documentation, and communication.

_____ 6. See what you can get from equipment manufacturers—before the account rep disappears.

_____ 7. Investigate training possibilities that may be available through colleges and universities.

_____ 8. Don't overlook your local school district's adult school.

_____ 9. Devise a way of building quality into the outsider's work. Set standards of quality regarding employee competency, product quality, and the quality of development processes.

_____ 10. Monitor the quality design and development of your project (in addition to monitoring the overall project implementation).

_____ 11. Use professional associations and journals as sources of contact persons, professional services, and information about the latest products in training.

CHAPTER 8

How to Get Around the Need for Training in the First Place

Training is required when individuals lack the specific skills or knowledge necessary to perform their jobs well. Done right, training is a powerful tool for enhancing productivity and encouraging personal growth. But in the big picture of an organization, it often comes at the expense of time. Training consumes the essential resource of time, especially in its planning, development, delivery, and integration phases. Even the most efficient training—the kind you now know how to do—might be more costly in time than some other solution to your personnel problems.

From what you have learned, you are now in a position to think about what's involved in training in a more informed way, to see more clearly what your options are regarding training design and delivery, and even to create or sponsor training that is cost-effective. This final chapter helps you to decide whether or not to choose training as your solution.

There are alternatives to training—those often hidden possibilities for solutions to human resources problems—that might not be as obvious to you as training is. This chapter suggests ways around the need for training in the first place, thus helping you to reserve training for only those times when training is the best choice.

Included are brief comments about recruiting, interviewing, selection, and placement; job design and performance monitoring; communicating, dealing with stress, managing change, and solving problems; and implementing policies and business plans. Often, problems identified in any of these areas can best be solved not by training but by a strategy that comes from the area itself and does not have the kind of carefully structured design and delivery requirements that go along with training. Save training for when you really need it.

The key to managing and developing the human resources in your organization is your analytical skills, your ability to zero in on the problem and its cause. Coupled with this is your ability to figure out what the elements of the solution are. Training often seems to be the ideal solution, but it may not be the correct solution if your problems are really not problems of skill or knowledge deficiency. People problems often occur when standards are not clear, job roles conflict, rewards are scarce, customers complain, resources are in short supply, equipment is broken, communication has deteriorated, or attitudes are poor. It's well worth your while to look carefully in various places before you accept the premise that inadequate performance is always best solved by training.

When you do this, follow this simple analysis procedure:

1. Describe the performance as you see it now. Try to be objective. Write it down. You are probably in for some surprises. Don't accuse or defend; simply get the facts.
2. Define the characteristics (quantity, quality, cost, attitude) of the performance you'd like to see.
3. Define the gap between what you have now and the ideal. Describe the deficiency in terms that can be measured (amount, percentage, weeks, dollars, persons to contact).
4. Prioritize the elements of the gap. Identify what's most important, what's least important, and what's in between. Figure out what you have to do first, second, third.

5. Identify the causes of the problem and your options for a solution.
6. Choose the best solution option and begin methodically to solve each element of the deficiency, taking them one by one.

Looking at How Employees Enter Your Organization

Prevent training problems from arising by selecting the right person for the job. This goes for new hires, transferred employees, reassigned employees, and promoted employees. Recurring and increasingly complex training problems arise when the selection of personnel is faulty.

Recruiting

In recruiting, these are some key points to focus on:

• *Applicant quality regardless of the number of applicants.* Encourage recruiters to keep looking for high-quality candidates even in adverse market conditions, so you won't have to spend a lot of time training poorly qualified people.

• *Level of ability of applicant.* Encourage recruiters to certify the abilities of applicants. Be sure recruiters know what your standards are. Provide recruiters with skills/abilities checklists to make sure they find you good people who don't need training right away.

• *Necessary versus useful qualifications.* Be sure recruiters know the difference so that they can provide you with candidates who enter the organization with all the necessary qualifications to do the job. Be sure your recruiter informs you what other qualifications the applicant has that might prove useful to you at a later date. It's a disaster to lump these together. To avoid training problems at the start, try to recruit people who can begin productive work right away. Try to avoid hiring people only for their potential usefulness.

• *Situational variables*. Be sure your recruiter knows exactly what your situation is. For example, you need someone who can work well alone in a cubicle in addition to being skilled and qualified in the subject, or your work day begins at 6:30 A.M. and your new hire must be able to manage the commute. Be sure your recruiter knows the constraints of your particular job opening so that you don't end up with a misfit who won't turn into an acceptable performer with all the training in the world. Recruiters can't be expected to know the quirks of running your operation, so be sure you tell them before they recruit.

• *Organizational and corporate values*. Don't overlook the necessity of informing your recruiter about the business practices you value. For example, good teamwork is more important to you than individual excellence; consistency of performance is more critical than creativity; responsiveness to the customer has to be evident in all business processes. Applicants who could do the job may nevertheless not share these values or have any interest in working within your particular organization. Be sure your recruiter knows how to qualify candidates on these items as well as on job skills.

Interviewing

Whether you or a personnel representative are doing the interviewing, focus on these points:

• *Consistency*. Use the same set of questions for all applicants and interview them for roughly the same amount of time. If peer interviews or multiple interviews are your practice, be sure all interviewers operate within the same structure in order to be fair to the applicant and to provide yourself with useful information. If you fall into inconsistent patterns of interviewing, you may easily overlook important aspects of the applicant's background that could spell big dollars in training later on.

• *Weighing negatives*. It seems to be human nature for interviewers when they write up an interview to highlight or spend more time describing an applicant's negative characteristics. Be sure these negatives are fairly documented in relationship to the applicant's positive characteristics. After all, it's basically the positives you're after, so be sure you give them their due when you write up your interview report.

• *Your time tolerance threshold.* Beware of your own frustration and exhaustion thresholds regarding the interview process. If you need to hire many people, as in a start-up operation, be sure to allow enough time to adequately interview each candidate. Plan ahead; schedule interviews so that you don't become tired or feel as if you're taking up too much time. Always measure by the same yardstick—and that includes your attitudes, emotional state, and the structure of the questions you ask. After you've hired someone, it's too late to find out that you missed an important element of that person's ability— or inability—and that only a crash course or expensive consultant can fix up the deficiency.

• *Job analysis.* Be sure you know what the applicant will be required to do in this particular job. Be realistic. Don't interview for an idealized job or on the basis of a job description that was written up three years ago. Look for a good match of employee to job, not for a superperson. Have sufficient job data on hand so that you can be very specific and clear with the applicant.

Selection

Avoid training problems by using thorough selection procedures and adequate selection variables. The following list contains variables on which individuals can distinguish themselves. During the employee selection process, isolate the characteristics in a person's background that indicate to you that this person is already well prepared to "hit the ground running" in your particular job. Remember, you're looking for ways to get around the need for training. As you follow your company's guidelines for interviewing and selection, always keep training requirements in the forefront of your thinking. Your goal is to select the best person for the job. Look for distinguishing characteristics in these areas:

- College/high school class rank
- Writing sample or test of written expression (if applicable to the job)
- Biographical data
- Work experience information
- Work sampling through "assessment center" job sample exercises
- Performance record on previous work
- Career goals

When you analyze the data you collect prior to selection, be aware that salary level and length of time spent in previous employment are often misrepresented. If you check references, be sure you ask probing questions such as "How does this person deal with deadlines?" or "How does this person go about solving problems?" or "Would you hire this person for a position higher than the one he had with your company?" Realize that the reference is likely to be biased. Ask enough questions of the reference to be sure that you won't immediately need to send your new hire off to training or play catch-up with him by doing the training yourself.

Placement

Accurate placement is the ultimate test of all the entry functions in an organization. Correctly placed employees don't need training in order to be productive. These are items to consider during placement:

- *Role expectations*. Be sure the new employee knows what's expected in terms of attitudes, knowledge, and skills.
- *Recognition and rewards*. Be sure that you explain the recognition and reward incentives very carefully and that the new employee can buy into them.
- *Support*. Be sure that the new employee has the support (clerical, graphic, building and grounds, legal, medical, library, supervisory, peer) necessary to do the job.

- *Job security.* Be sure that the new employee has a sense that her job is important and will be around for a while.
- *The job itself.* Be sure that the new employee has demonstrated that he can do the job.

Analyzing the Work Itself

Sometimes what appears to be a training problem is actually a problem with the design of the job: The job itself may have evolved over time so that it is now too easy or too hard for most people; the pay may be unrealistic; technology may have made the job more of a challenge, more efficient, or just plain different from what it was; or, the job itself may never have been what you thought it was. Sometimes looking at the design of the job through performance monitoring in a systematic way or through the analysis of documents (sales figures, profit and loss statements, customer complaints, inventory, standards, and specifications) can help you to see how the job itself might be modified so as to encourage better performance. A performance problem might be a job design problem, not a training problem. And if you apply training to a job design problem, chances are you'll be wasting everyone's time.

Job Design

These are some elements to be aware of in job design; quite possibly they can be changed to bring about a desired change in employee performance:

- *Specificity of procedures.* Be sure procedures are specific and clear. Most employees can and will follow directions that are appropriate, specific, and clearly stated.
- *Complexity of rules.* Look for rules that are unduly complicated and make them simpler. Sometimes corporate gurus get carried away with lofty sounding rules that simply don't work in practice or don't apply to the job in question. A good rule of

thumb is to break down rules into smaller parts when they seem outrageous or too complex. Give employees a chance to demonstrate small successes and to accumulate them. It's less frustrating to follow many small rules than to give up over trying to figure out a few complicated ones.

• *Flow of work*. Look at the way work passes through the organization and be sure it flows smoothly without any hangups. Often what appears to be a training problem is really an obstacle in the flow of work.

• *Division of labor*. Check the organization chart and the responsibilities of employees in the unit to which this job belongs. Check the productivity records for employees with similar jobs; check the expectations of persons with whom this employee comes in contact; get a sense of reality regarding the volume of work and the interdependencies among employees who affect this job. Sometimes a person simply has too much work or too little work, and the way the work is divided up among colleagues in that unit has to be changed before productivity can improve. A change in the division of labor in a unit often erases the perceived need for training. Think how bad it would be to "throw training" at a person who is already overworked or overstressed by having too many subordinates!

• *People/data/things*. A problem in job design can arise when an employee is called upon to perform a job that has slowly changed from one kind of emphasis to another. This can be described as a people/data/things dissonance. It occurs, for example, when a job that was originally characterized largely by people interactions has changed over time to one that is characterized by a dependence on data, or when a job that was data-dependent is subsequently taken over by a machine (thing).

A typical situation is that of the personnel specialist who originally held consultations with eight or ten job applicants per day but who now, because of new federal regulations regarding drug testing, affirmative action, and a host of other requirements, can see only two applicants per day, the rest of her day being needed for filling out paperwork. In this situation, the job design has changed and the employee feels a dissonance between the "people" nature of the job, which she prefers, and the "data" nature of the job, which she detests.

As you look at job design, look for the kinds of dissonance that might be bothering employees. Training will not make that personnel specialist a better worker if she really can't stand to do the job as it is now configured. Changing that employee's assignment might be the only solution to the problem.

Performance Monitoring

Performance monitoring and performance reviews are excellent sources of information about knowledge and skill deficiencies that require remedial attention. These techniques are also good sources for uncovering other, non-training, solutions to performance problems.

The kind of performance appraisal that most employees go through with their supervisors is the annual or semiannual review in which the various elements of their performance are rated on a scale ranging from unsatisfactory to outstanding. Sometimes, a detailed breakdown of job parts or demonstrated skills is made. Weights are assigned depending on how important a particular skill is to the job, and what the employee's rating or score is on a 1-to-5, low-to-high scale for each skill. Training is often a suggested, and generally appropriate, way of upgrading anything that is documented as a skill deficiency.

But sometimes as you go through a performance monitoring or appraisal process, you find that the cause of poor performance or of a skill deficiency is a health problem (for example, a bad back), a lack of resources to do the job (for example, broken equipment), or a personal problem at home. In situations like these, training won't solve the deficiency problem. The important thing is to look beyond the results on the rating scale to find out why the performance is lacking. Often the preferred solution will lead you in an entirely different direction from the one in which training would have led you, and in the end it will be a whole lot better for the employee as well as the business.

Processes That Sustain or Undermine Progress

As a manager, you probably have a pretty good idea of how your organization runs—that is, what the dynamics of the group are, how people support each other or shoot each other down, how communications are passed from peer to peer and up and down the line, how much it takes to overcome inertia, how innovative your group is, what pressures it responds to, and what kind of group image it projects to the rest of the company. Often, a closer look at some of these group processes uncovers problems that can be solved very quickly and inexpensively— problems that you might otherwise have tried to solve through training.

Communicating

The essentials of good communication are quality input, quality processing, quality output, and quality feedback. These four parts of any communication system are the places to look for potential problems. It's tempting to look only at the output message or to listen to the negative feedback, but that's selling yourself short. Go back to the beginning and look at the original message for accuracy, clarity, relevance, and timing. Then look at the processing. Are the channels the right ones? Are they working well? Is there noise or distortion in the transmission process? Then look at how the message came out on the receiving end, and weigh all feedback. Often a simple change in any part of the communication will produce dramatically improved results. The secret is to see each part and to refrain from jumping to the conclusion that a person needs training because he got the wrong message or didn't get any message.

Dealing With Stress

The kind of stress that comes from the job itself may have many causes, and often these causes can be eliminated. Managers who fail to look into the job, however, all too often send stressed employees off to career workshops, time management courses, stress reduction seminars, and other inappropriate forms of training.

Dealing with stress often means examining people's motivation for work—that is, examining how the results of work are valued by the organization and by you, what the rewards and punishments of work are, what the employee's needs for power, security, and achievement are, and whether the employee can do the work. Dealing with stress often means altering motivational factors—for example, removing punishments, recasting the reward formulas, making achievement more visible, cleaning up a threat to safety, buying new software, making the job easier through more support. Find out what bugs people, and get rid of the bugs. Don't treat the symptom with training; go for the cure.

Managing Change

Viable organizations are ones that know that change is a part of life and must be managed systematically. Managers who allow themselves to become defensive about change or who fulfill only the role of reactor to change could run the risk of pursuing too much training or training for the wrong reasons. As you think about why an employee is not performing, think about the nature of the changes that are currently going on in your organization.

Think, too, about the specific ways in which those changes affect your employees. Look for ways to help them understand the change, see their positive contributions to it, identify options for dealing with it, and realize some benefits from the change. Don't assume that an employee needs training in order to cope with change; sometimes all you need to do is to sit down for an hour and explain things and listen with concern to that employee. Your ability to give guidance in this situation is far more important than your ability to train or get training for this person.

Solving Problems

Much is made of the ability of managers to solve problems. To be sure, problems are part of every manager's daily work, and solved problems are a boon to any manager. The thing to realize is that problems have many causes, and the need for training is only one of them. Don't assume that training will solve all your problems.

To be a problem-solving manager who sees training in its proper perspective, be consistent and methodical in your approach to problems. Think of there being two fundamental parts to a problem, the "problem finding" part and the "solution finding" part. In this way you can isolate the elements that might benefit from training in either the problem-finding part or the solution-finding part.

The first structured task in problem finding is fact finding. In this phase you seek information about what is currently happening. It involves separating fact from assumption and distinguishing between actual outcomes and idealized guidelines and standards. Finding a problem is an exercise in definition and description. Sometimes what seems to be the problem is really not the problem. Taking the time to find the real problem can lead to its speedy solution.

During fact finding, the manager generates ideas as to why the problem occurred and where the sources of difficulty lie. This focusing on the problem and hypothesizing propels the problem-solving process forward. In problem finding, the manager goes through the exercise of giving weight to certain ideas, of organizing information in a hierarchy, of building a case for certain kinds of action.

Solution finding begins with uncovering what has to change in order for the problem to go away. Solution finding involves specifying the small steps in a work procedure that need to be done differently. Solution finding considers options regarding the best way. Good problem solvers will ask the questions, "Is the problem worth solving? What are the costs? What are the benefits? Is the solution practical and doable? Is this solution a priority? What will the consequences be if we don't solve this problem?" Good problem solvers will come up with a list of several ways of solving a problem. From the list of plausible options, the best one will be chosen, and the organization will be on its way to accomplishing the change it seeks.

Lining Up Business Practices With Business Directives

Sometimes the boardroom and executive offices seem far away from the line worker, the account rep, the engineer, the secretary, and even the manager. As a manager, you go along doing your job the best way you can. What happens when the way you're doing your job seems a little out of synch with what's coming down from the top? Chances are that you give at least a little thought to the possibility that either you or your employees might need some training when the way you are currently doing business varies from expected practices as reflected in executive directives.

Be careful. The source of your problems might not be related to training at all; instead, your timing might be off, communication channels might be cluttered, your old biases might be getting in your way, or you might simply lack information. Try to step back and define what the components of your problems are, and look for plausible solutions. Chances are that this kind of "alignment" problem doesn't require a training solution.

Implementing Policies

When your employees' performance (or your own) starts to deteriorate, look first to the company's personnel policies to see what the corporate value system really is. Your way of doing business as usual may be in direct conflict with a policy regarding rotation, career counseling, job enlargement, or certifying promotability. Checking policies like these that are written down somewhere, and that your employees have access to, could lead to pinpointing the source of the misaligned behavior. In most such cases, getting back on track is a relatively simple matter. Some training may be called for, but check other sources and solutions before you make that decision.

Implementing Business Plans

Your company may have several layers of business plans—one for the company as a whole, one for each vice-presidential area of responsibility, and one for each separate operational function. To look for the source of performance problems, go first to the top layer. Gather up and read the business plans for each layer in your chain of command. Look for clear, consistent threads that make sense to you in terms of your operation and the people who work for you.

Look for planning goals on the first page of these plans in sections that are usually called "Goals," "Reasons for the Plan," "Strategies," or "Objectives." Look for statements that sound similar. Look especially for statements in the lowest-level plan that are inconsistent with statements in the higher-level plans.

Look at those sections of the business plans that present an analysis of markets, customers, profits, and business opportunities to be sure that you are working within the same framework and that you understand what the percentages and numbers mean. Look at timelines, control points, and resource requirements to be sure they make sense to you. Fixing up a performance problem might mean modifying a business plan so that implementing that business plan becomes easier and more in line with other corporate goals. Or it could mean modifying individual practices to bring them into greater conformity with the overall business plan.

For example, a salesperson who is not meeting quotas might get a boost from a business plan that clearly defines quotas in a less stringent way. Overzealous employees are sometimes tempted to jeopardize their health when they don't know what the directives are for the business as a whole. If you don't look at the directives/practices alignment issue, you may be tempted to prescribe sales training for that salesperson when it is actually not needed.

In Brief

Save training for solutions to performance problems that result from skill or knowledge deficiencies. Keep your eyes and ears open for the many other areas of business practice that might be out of line. Take action to fix these other areas and thus get around the need for developing and delivering what could be costly training. In this chapter I have suggested places to find solutions to human resources problems that lie outside the realm of training. Training is an excellent option for increasing productivity and facilitating personal growth, but it should only be selected for the right reasons.

The following checklist helps show you what those right reasons are and suggests other business practices that might provide a simpler solution to your human resources problems.

MANAGER'S CHECKLIST 8

How to Get Around the Need for Training in the First Place

_____   1. Be sure the recruiting, interviewing, selecting, and placing of employees is carefully matched to your particular job opening. Work with your personnel specialists to prevent training problems from arising as employees enter your organization.

_____   2. Look at the design of the job to be sure that the way it is being done is the way it was designed to be done. Poor performance sometimes results from a flaw in the design of the job.

_____   3. Check out your communication process to be sure all parts are working well—sending inputs, processing or transmitting messages, receiving outputs, and providing feedback. Substandard performance often results from poor communication.

_____   4. Examine what the sources of stress are for your employees.

_____   5. Help your employees manage change.

_____   6. Apply a structured methodology to defining and solving problems.

_____   7. Analyze corporate policies and business plans so that you can align your practices with corporate directives.

_____   8. Aim good training at the right target.

Bibliography

Alessi, S. M., and S. R. Trollip. *Computer-Based Instruction Methods and Development*. Englewood Cliffs, N.J.: Prentice Hall, 1985.

Birnbaum, H., ed. *Handbook for Technical and Skills Training*. Alexandria, Va.: ASTD, 1985.

Bloom, B. S., ed. *Taxonomy of Educational Objectives, Handbook I: Cognitive Domain*. New York: Longman, 1954.

Gagne, R. M., and L. J. Briggs. *Principles of Instructional Design*. New York: Holt, Rinehart & Winston, 1979.

Gilbert, T. F. *Human Competence*. New York: McGraw-Hill, 1978.

Mager, R. F., and P. Pipe. *Analyzing Performance Problems, or 'You Really Oughta Wanna.'* Belmont, Calif.: Fearon Pitman, 1970.

National Society for Performance and Instruction (NSPI). *Introduction to Performance Technology, Vol. 1*. Washington, D.C. 1986.

Nilson, C. *Training Program Workbook and Kit*. Englewood Cliffs, N.J.: Prentice Hall, 1989.

Perkins, D. N. *Knowledge as Design*. Hillside, N.J.: Lawrence Erlbaum, 1986.

Rossett, A. *Training Needs Assessment*. Englewood Cliffs, N.J.: Educational Technology Publications, 1987.

Simpson, E. J. *The Classification of Objectives, Psychomotor Domain*. Urbana, Ill.: University of Illinois, 1966.

Tracey, W. R. *Designing Training and Development Systems*. New York: AMACOM, 1984.

Index